MAD
ABOUT
FOOD
THE COOKBOOK

CW00937621

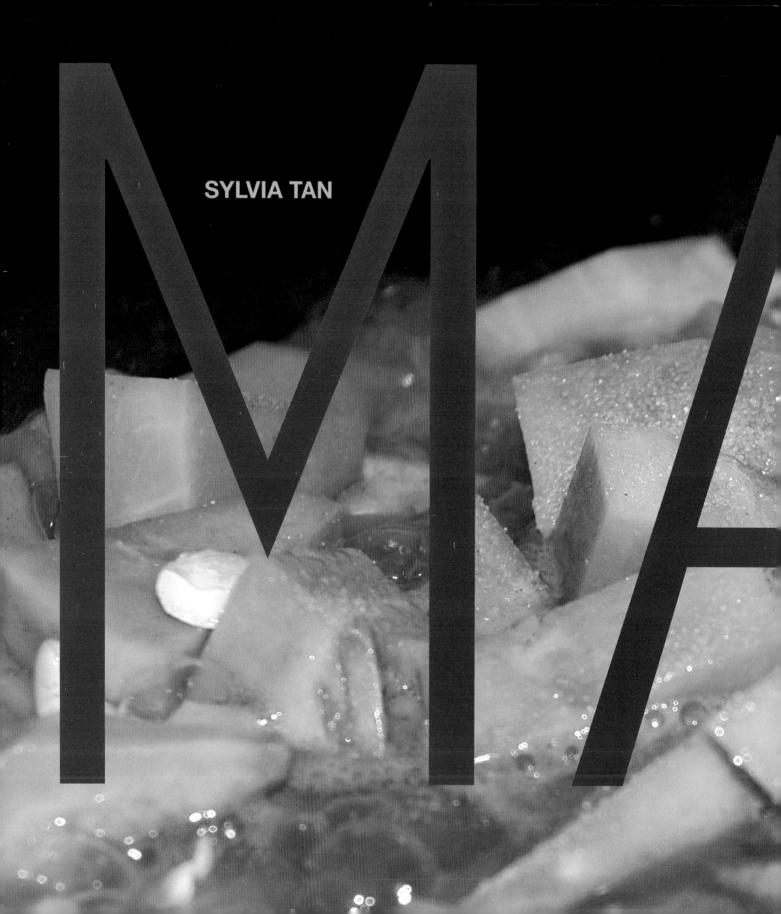

SYLVIA TAN

ABOUT
FOOD
THE COOKBOOK

 **Marshall Cavendish**
Cuisine

The Publisher wishes to thank Lim's Arts and Living Pte Ltd for the loan of their tableware.

Designer   :   Chris Wong
Photographer :   Joshua Tan, Little Black Box

Text © 2005 Sylvia Tan
Photographs © 2005 Marshall Cavendish International (Asia) Private Limited

Published by Marshall Cavendish Cuisine
An imprint of Marshall Cavendish International
1 New Industrial Road, Singapore 536196

All rights reserved

No part of this publication may be reproduced, stored in a retrieval system or transmitted, in any form or by any means, electronic, mechanical, photocopying, recording or otherwise, without the prior permission of the copyright owner. Request for permission should be addressed to the Publisher, Marshall Cavendish International (Asia) Private Limited, 1 New Industrial Road, Singapore 536196. Tel: (65) 6213 9300, fax: (65) 6285 4871. E-mail: te@sg.marshallcavendish.com

Limits of Liability/Disclaimer of Warranty: The Author and Publisher of this book have used their best efforts in preparing this book. The Publisher makes no representation or warranties with respect to the contents of this book and is not responsible for the outcome of any recipe in this book. While the Publisher has reviewed each recipe carefully, the reader may not always achieve the results desired due to variations in ingredients, cooking temperatures and individual cooking abilities. The Publisher shall in no event be liable for any loss of profit or any other commercial damage, including but not limited to special, incidental, consequential, or other damages

Other Marshall Cavendish Offices:

Marshall Cavendish Ltd. 119 Wardour Street, London W1F OUW, UK • Marshall Cavendish Corporation. 99 White Plains Road, Tarrytown NY 10591-9001, USA • Marshall Cavendish International (Thailand) Co Ltd. 253 Asoke, 12th Flr, Sukhumvit 21 Road, Klongtoey Nua, Wattana, Bangkok 10110, Thailand • Marshall Cavendish (Malaysia) Sdn Bhd, Times Subang, Lot 46, Subang Hi-Tech Industrial Park, Batu Tiga, 40000 Shah Alam, Selangor Darul Ehsan, Malaysia

Marshall Cavendish is a trademark of Times Publishing Limited

National Library Board Singapore Cataloguing in Publication Data

Tan, Sylvia.
Mad about food : the cookbook / Sylvia Tan. – Singapore : Marshall Cavendish Cuisine, c2005.
p. cm.
Includes index.
ISBN : 981-261-203-3

1. Cookery. I. Title.

TX714
641.5 -- dc21   SLS2005042847

Printed in Singapore by Tien Wah Press Pte Ltd

For my father,
Heng Cheng,
my first cooking
mentor

ACKNOWLEDGEMENTS

Cooks need people around them who like food. For me, they are the ones who have influenced, inspired and encouraged me to keep on cooking.

My earliest culinary mentors are my father and grandmother. From my dad comes that gift of being able to taste something and replicate it later in the kitchen; from my grandmother comes that entire heritage of Peranakan cooking, which is in my blood and rules my taste buds.

Then there is my circle of friends, all mad about food, on whom I can always count to discuss an ingredient or a new way of doing things.

My sisters-in-law, Barbara, whom I cook with regularly and with much pleasure, and Anne, for being my super support especially during the photography for this book.

Finally, the men in my life—Kay Tong, my husband, and Yeun Cheong, my son. Without the both of you, I would never have developed this passion that now thoroughly shapes and fulfills my life.

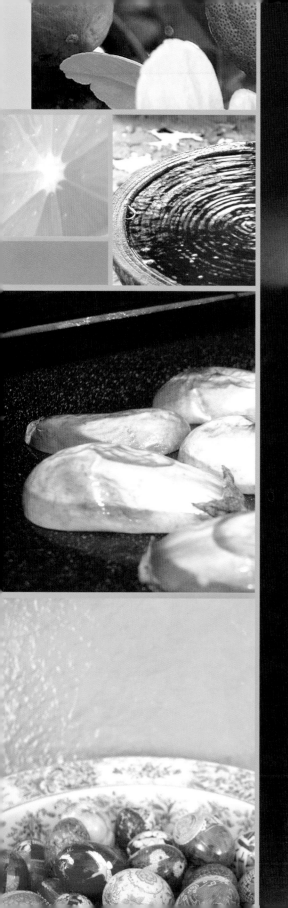

INTRODUCTION

These are my favourite recipes. Reading them, you will get a glimpse into the kind of food I like to serve my friends and family and hopefully, you will enjoy it as much as they do.

They will, after all, unhesitatingly call me and ask me to turn out once again the Burmese tea leaf salad that I once served them or the Keralan chicken that I wrote about, or a family favourite, spaghetti using Chinese salted fish to flavour the noodles.

You will gather from all these that I love cooking, though it must be said that not for me is the kind of cooking that takes hours to prepare or demands mincing preparations.

I'm afraid I am too impatient by nature.

Instead, I like to take a traditional recipe and see if I can make it easier and less of a hassle for a busy modern cook. You will find many shortcuts in this book, although the purists will pooh-pooh such attempts!

That said, some things are better left unchanged and so, a granite mortar and pestle is still part of my battery of kitchen equipment. Nothing can beat the taste of fresh *sambal belacan* being turned out by sheer sweat and picking up the leavings later with just rice and a swirl of hot oil to obtain fiery *nasi lesong*!

I also cook most often in a well-seasoned wok and steam in an old-fashioned stacked bamboo steamer, although, at the same time, the food chopper and microwave oven are also equally used.

The recipes are well-tested as I make them often in my kitchen. However, if I do not give an exact measurement, do not panic, it merely means that you can add more or less as you like. A lot of cooking depends on individual taste and I would like to encourage you to taste along the way so that you can adjust accordingly. Indeed, if you watch real cooks, this is what they do, dunk a finger into the pot and lick it to see if it suits theirs and no one else's taste buds!

You will also find suggestions on how to match dishes and how to serve a meal. While taste is paramount, eating is more than just filling one's stomach. The eye must be pleased as well as the taste buds, and no one wants to be assaulted with too much of a good thing which is what successful meal planning is all about.

Indeed, food is about good taste in all the senses so, a meal well-cooked and chosen and beautifully served is a true gift to loved ones.

Sylvia Tan

FAMILY

Cooking for the family, at least mine, calls for gutsy, filling food with flavours turned up several notches!

You do not need gussied-up presentations, but you do need quantity, spice, meat and lots of delicious gravy for the rice to sop up! This is the kind of casual eating I love where we can all dig in using fingers and no one cares.

On such days, invariably weekends, I try to offer a big pot of something that hits the spot—spicy is good—white rice and yes, greens which I will serve everyone, even the teenagers! And if there is to be a salad, I may bring out one of my Asian dressed salads to suit the Asian taste buds, which can be resolutely unswerving! Dessert can be just local fruit in season, ice cream and, if I feel energetic, perhaps a pudding.

Roti Babi

(For 6–8)

I have a secret passion for crisp-fried foods… and *roti babi,* with its mound of deliciously flavoured meat sitting on crisp bread, is something I would bite into when I feel a snack attack coming on.

Ingredients

Minced pork (or chicken)	300 g (10½ oz)
Onion	1, large, peeled and finely chopped
Egg	1
Corn flour (cornstarch)	1 tsp
Salt	½ tsp
Ground white pepper	to taste
Fresh water chestnuts	4–5, peeled and chopped
Vegetable oil for deep-frying	
Day-old white bread slices	8
Worcestershire sauce	
Sliced red chillies	

Method

❖ Mix minced pork (or chicken) with chopped onion. Bind with egg and corn flour. Season with salt and pepper to taste. Add water chestnuts for a bit of crunch.

❖ Heat wok half full with oil. In the meantime, spread meat mixture evenly on each slice of bread. Now, test if oil is hot enough by tossing in a small piece of bread. It should sizzle.

❖ Carefully slide bread, meat side down, into hot oil and fry until golden. Turn over to fry other side until golden.

❖ Remove and drain on absorbent paper. Serve hot, with a dip of Worcestershire sauce spiked as desired, with fresh red chillies.

Note

Worcestershire sauce or *ang moh tau yu* (literally "Caucasian soy sauce") is a 19th century English sauce made by using a base of shallots, anchovies, vinegar, sugar, light soy sauce, tamarind, ginger, cloves, nutmeg and cardamom. It is an essential accompaniment for Asian dishes such as fried chicken (*inchee kabin*) and yes, *roti babi.*

Killer Prawns

(For 8–10)

When I have truly fresh prawns (shrimps), I like to cook them in this spicy broth that is scalp-tingling spicy. I serve it in huge bowls, accompanied by crusty bread. The idea is to dunk the bread into the broth and tackle the prawns with fingers.

Ingredients

Prawns (shrimps)	1 kg (2 lb 3 oz), medium-sized
Water	2 litres (64 fl oz / 8 cups)
Olive oil	4 Tbsp
Onions	2, peeled and chopped
Garlic	2 cloves, peeled and chopped
Tomato	1, chopped
Mixed dried herbs (oregano, rosemary and basil leaves)	2 Tbsp
Dried chilli flakes	1 Tbsp, or more if you like it spicier
White wine	2 Tbsp
Italian parsley or Chinese celery	2–3 stalks, chopped
Crusty French bread	

Method

- To make prawn stock, remove heads of prawns and set prawns aside. Dry-fry heads until fragrant and roasted. Add water and bring to the boil. This forms the basis of your broth.
- Meanwhile, heat olive oil in a wok and brown onions and garlic until softened. Add chopped tomato, dried herbs and chilli flakes according to taste. Add white wine. Pour prawn stock over and bring to the boil.
- Add prawns. When prawn stock returns to the boil, remove from heat.
- Ladle into individual bowls and garnish with chopped parsley or Chinese celery. Serve immediately with crusty bread.

Indonesian Barbecued Spare Ribs

(For 8–10)

My family loves barbecued ribs. Done Indonesian style, the meat is parboiled after which, a marinade is smeared all over before the meat is seared over the grill. This is not only delicious, it also obviates the perennial worry of raw meat at barbecues.

Ingredients

Rack of ribs	2–3 kg (4 lb 6 oz–6 lb 9 oz)
Salt	1 tsp

Marinade

Lemon grass	1 stalk
Tamarind pulp	1 tsp, mixed with 4 Tbsp water and strained
Thick dark soy sauce	125 ml (4 fl oz / 1/2 cup)
Sweet flour sauce (*tee cheo*)	125 ml (4 fl oz / 1/2 cup)
Chopped red chilli	2 Tbsp
Vegetable oil	2 Tbsp
Salt	1 tsp

Method

- Choose pork or beef prime ribs. They are substantial and meaty. Rub salt into rack of ribs and parboil for about 15 minutes in a pot of water. Remove ribs. (Save stock for use in another dish.)
- Heat up grill or barbecue.
- Meanwhile, place all ingredients for marinade except salt in a pot and heat until it thickens slightly. Stir in salt. Leave marinade to cool, then add parboiled ribs to marinate for about 15 minutes.
- When grill is hot, turn down heat to medium. Brush some oil over grill racks. Place ribs on grill and baste frequently while cooking. The ribs should be done in about 15 minutes. Slice between bones to separate ribs and serve.

Tip

Eat this with white rice and *sambal belacan* (chilli with toasted prawn (shrimp) paste) mixed with chopped tomatoes and some hot oil.

Turmeric Chicken

(For 8 as part of a meal)

Tired of eating chicken curry? Try this one-spice chicken, flavoured with just turmeric. The root spice softens upon cooking and yields a tasty and uncomplicated dish.

Ingredients

Chicken	1, about 1.5 kg (3 lb 4$^1/_2$ oz)
Vegetable oil	4 Tbsp
Onion	1, peeled and chopped
Garlic	2 cloves, peeled and chopped
Ginger	1 thumb-sized knob, peeled and chopped
Ground turmeric	1 Tbsp
Salt	2 Tbsp
Ground white pepper	to taste
Potatoes	5–6, peeled and cut into large pieces
Coconut milk	500 ml (16 fl oz / 2 cups)

Method

- Cut chicken into 8–10 pieces. Pat dry with absorbent paper.
- Heat oil in a pot. Sauté onion, garlic and ginger until fragrant, then add ground turmeric, made first into a paste with a little water.
- When oil rises in the pot, add chicken pieces and cook until brown.
- Add water to reach to half of chicken. Season with salt and pepper. Bring to the boil, then add potatoes. Turn down heat to simmer until chicken and potatoes are tender.
- Add coconut milk. Stir constantly until stew returns to a gentle boil to prevent milk from curdling. Taste to adjust seasoning, if necessary.
- Serve with white rice and salted egg cucumber salad (see pg 76).

Note

When reference is made to "thumb-sized" knobs of root spice, it means that the exact amount of spice is not critical. Just add as you like.

Keralan **Chicken Roast**
(For 8)

This is another spicy chicken dish, this time from Kerala. It is sweet with onions and spices, and uses raw cashews and dried raisins as finishing notes.

Ingredients

Chicken parts	1.5 kg (3 lb 4$\frac{1}{2}$ oz)
Chilli powder	1 tsp
Ground turmeric	1 tsp
Salt	1 Tbsp
Vegetable oil	4 Tbsp
Garlic	1 head, peeled and chopped
Ginger	1 thumb-sized knob, peeled and chopped
Purple onions	8–10, peeled and sliced
Tomatoes	2, chopped
Green chillies	4–5, chopped
Ground coriander	1 Tbsp
Raw cashew nuts and raisins	1 cup
Garam masala	1 tsp

Method

- Strip chicken of skin and fat. The market stallholders will do this for you, if requested. Rub chilli powder and ground turmeric into chicken. Season with salt. Leave to marinate for 15–20 minutes.

- Heat oil in a wok and sauté garlic and ginger. Add onions, tomatoes and chillies.

- When softened, add chicken and brown. Turn down heat and cook covered, turning now and then until chicken is tender and sauce thickens. Do not add any liquid to wok. The onion and chicken juices will cook the meat until tender.

- Halfway through, add ground coriander, cashew nuts and raisins. Cook for another 15 minutes or until chicken is cooked and tender.

- Stir in garam masala at the end and serve with white rice and a plain salad.

Tip

The South Indians do a chopped salad of tomato, cucumber, carrot, celery, beetroot and onion, dressed simply with oil, lemon juice, salt and pepper, which is an excellent counterpoint to this chicken dish.

Dry Chilli Crab
(For 4–6)

This fried crab is definitely finger-licking good! It is sweet with onions, tangy with tomato and tingling hot with chilli powder and turmeric.

Ingredients

Live mud crabs or flower crabs	3, medium-sized and male, if possible
Vegetable oil	125 ml (4 fl oz / 1/2 cup)
Onion	1, large, peeled and sliced
Garlic	2–3 cloves, peeled and sliced
Ginger	1 thumb-sized knob, peeled and shredded
Chilli powder	1 Tbsp
Ground turmeric	1 tsp
Tomatoes	2, cut into quarters
Salt	1 tsp
Sugar	1/2 tsp
White wine	

Method

- If using live mud crabs, place in the freezer for 30 minutes to put them to sleep.
- Now proceed with the rest of the recipe for either type of crab. Scrub them clean of dirt and encrusted mud. Pull off main shell, discard brown gills within, remove stomach bag and bottom flap.
- Pull out pincers and cut body, legs attached, into 2 or 4 parts, depending on the size of crab. Use a pestle to crack mud crab pincers, to allow sauce to penetrate.
- Heat oil in a wok and fry crab pieces for a couple of minutes until they change colour.
- Remove crabs, then brown onion, garlic and ginger in the same oil. Add a little water to chilli powder and ground turmeric to make a paste. Fry paste gently until oil rises. Add tomatoes and more oil, if needed.
- Put crabs back into wok. Add salt and sugar. Toss to ensure an even mix of spices and seasoning. Moisten with a splash of white wine and cover to cook for a few minutes.
- If crabs seem too dry, add a little water to moisten.

Tip

There are a couple of options to cooking crabs. You could cook them first before finishing them in the sauce, or you could cook both crabs and sauce together. I prefer the first way because cooking the crabs and sauce together can cause the spices to burn while waiting for the crabs to cook.

Ayam **Plecing**
(For 4–5)

This is a spicy chicken salad from Lombok. It is so simple to prepare, it has no business to taste so good! This recipe comes in handy when you have leftover roast chicken (or even turkey). Just shred the meat and toss it in this warm chilli-tomato dressing.

Ingredients

Vegetable oil	2–3 Tbsp
Tomatoes	2, chopped
Roast chicken meat	3–4 cups, shredded
Salt	a pinch
Limes	2, cut into wedges

Spice paste

Red chillies	10–12, seeded, if you prefer the dish less spicy
Onions	2, medium-sized, peeled and roughly chopped
Garlic	5 cloves, peeled
Belacan (dried prawn (shrimp) paste)	1 Tbsp

29
MAD
ABOUT
FOOD
THE COOKBOOK

Method

* To make spice paste, place chillies, onions, garlic and *belacan* in a food processor and chop until fine. Store paste in a jar in the refrigerator or freezer, if keeping for more than a few days, before cooking.

* Heat oil in a wok and brown spice paste over low heat until fragrant and caramelised. Add chopped tomatoes and cook until they meld into sauce. Add a bit of water if it seems too dry. What you are aiming for is a sauce with lots of lovely red chilli oil in it.

* Toss shredded chicken meat in this flavoursome chilli dressing. Season with salt to taste.

* Squeeze lime juice over just before serving.

* Serve with plain white rice (or use as a sandwich filling with bread) and some lightly cooked greens (broccoli or Chinese broccoli (Chinese kale)), stir-fried or even poached in the stock made by boiling the chicken carcass from the roast chicken.

Chilli Crab Linguini

(For 6–8)

All the favourite flavours of Singapore chilli crab can be found in this wicked pasta sauce, which makes it more convenient for the diner (not the cook!) to enjoy chilli crab! It is made with picked crabmeat.

Ingredients

Mud crabs or flower crabs	3, large, to get 2–3 cups crabmeat
Light olive oil	125 ml (4 fl oz / $^1/_2$ cup)
Brown onions	2, peeled and chopped
Ripe tomatoes	3, chopped
Chopped garlic	1 tsp
Dried chilli flakes	1 Tbsp
Brown soy bean paste (*tau cheo*)	1 rounded (heaped) Tbsp
Sugar	1 Tbsp
Salt	1 tsp or to taste
Light soy sauce (optional)	
Dried linguini	500 g (1 lb 1$^1/_2$ oz)
Chopped Chinese celery	
Crusty French bread	

Method

- Bring a pot of salted water to the boil. Scrub crabs clean and when water is boiling, lower crabs in to cook for about 8 minutes, then turn off heat. Leave crabs to cool in the pot for 10 minutes.

- Remove crabs, set aside the pot of water, and pry off shells and hard bits in the middle, as well as the feathery gills.

- Save yellow 'mustard' or roe to add to sauce later. Cut body into 4 parts, then proceed to extract flesh, using nutcrackers, skewers or a pair of scissors.

- Leave crabmeat, covered, in the refrigerator until needed. This can be done a day ahead.

- Heat olive oil in a wok and sauté chopped onions, tomatoes and garlic until caramelised. Add dried chilli flakes.

- Now come the Asian touches. Add brown soy bean paste and sugar. Stir well, turn heat down and leave to simmer, adding water from cooking crabs from time to time, until flavours amalgamate. Add crabmeat and roe at the last moment.

- Season with salt to taste. If needed, add a drizzle of light soy sauce, which has a more complex saltiness.

- Bring the pot of water from cooking crabs to the boil and use it to cook the pasta. This will add more crab flavour. Add more water if needed. When boiling, put in linguini and cook until al dente or according to preference. Drain.

- Toss sauce with drained pasta and garnish with chopped Chinese celery. Serve with lots of crusty bread on the side to mop up, in time-honoured fashion, the delicious bits of chilli crab sauce.

Tip

Avoid using frozen packs of crabmeat as they are watery and tasteless. The best way is still to buy whole crabs, boil them and strip them clean. It is laborious and painstaking work, but well worth the effort.

Pork and Cencaluk Salad

(For 6–8 as part of a meal)

A luscious and traditional combination of belly pork, covered with sliced shallots and chilli, dressed with *cencaluk* (salted prawn (shrimp) sauce) and sharp lime juice. I salve my conscience when serving it by adding lots of greens!

Ingredients

Belly pork	200 g (7 oz)
Mixed salad leaves	1 packet, choose according to individual taste. I like any packet that includes the nutty rocket (arugula) leaf
Tomatoes	4, sliced
Cucumber	1, sliced
Red chillies	2, sliced
Onion	1, peeled and sliced

Dressing

Cencaluk (salted prawn (shrimp) sauce)	2 Tbsp, thinned down with 5 Tbsp water
Limes	5–6, squeezed for juice
Sesame oil	1 tsp
Sugar	2 tsp
Limes	2, grated for zest
Shallots	2–3, peeled and finely sliced

Method

- Boil pork in a pot of water until tender. Drain and save stock for use in another recipe. Slice pork thinly, then refrigerate until needed.

- Place salad leaves, tomatoes, cucumber, chillies and onions in a salad bowl. Top with pork slices.

- Place dressing ingredients in a bowl and use a fork to combine. Taste to adjust seasoning. Dress salad just before serving.

Grilled Vegetables in
Black Bean Marinade

(For 6–8 as part of a meal)

These grilled vegetables are truly Asian, marinated first in a fermented black bean oil, incidentally a classic match for vegetables such as capsicums and aubergines (eggplants/brinjals).

Ingredients

Red, orange and yellow capsicums (bell peppers)	3, one of each colour
Fermented black beans	2–3 Tbsp, chopped
Finely chopped red chillies	1 Tbsp
Chopped garlic	1 Tbsp
Peanut oil	125 ml (4 fl oz / $^1/_2$ cup)
Courgette (zucchini)	1, medium, cut into 1-cm ($^1/_2$-in) thick slices
Aubergine (eggplant/brinjal)	1, large, cut into 1-cm ($^1/_2$-in) thick slices
White onions	2, peeled and cut into wedges
Black rice vinegar	
Salt	a pinch
Ground white pepper	to taste

34
MAD
ABOUT
FOOD
THE COOKBOOK

Method

- Discard seeds and stems of capsicums. Cut them into quarters.
- Mix together chopped black beans, chillies and garlic with oil. Coat vegetables with this marinade and leave covered for 2–3 hours.
- Place vegetables under a really hot grill for about 15 minutes on each side or until they are slightly charred in parts.
- To serve, toss vegetables with black rice vinegar, salt and pepper.

Note

If you prefer to serve the salad as a meal, marinate some chicken pieces in the same sauce, then grill and serve together with the roasted vegetables. It makes for a salad that is robust enough for Asian tastes.

Coconut Bread Pudding
(For 10)

Actually a comfort food from the West, this is something we've adopted wholeheartedly and why not, especially when it is made with coconut milk and palm sugar. Besides, it is one dessert that appeals to my practical bent of mind for it conveniently uses up stale bread!

Ingredients

Screwpine (*pandan*) leaves	2–3, snipped into pieces
French bread or white bread	8, thick slices
Chopped palm sugar (*gula* Melaka)	1 cup
Eggs	6
Castor (superfine) sugar	1/2 cup
Coconut milk	500 ml (16 fl oz / 2 cups), mixed with 750 ml (24 fl oz / 3 cups) milk or soy milk
Rum (optional)	1 Tbsp

Syrup

Chopped palm sugar (*gula* Melaka)	1 cup
Water	250 ml (8 fl oz / 1 cup)
Coconut milk	125 ml (4 fl oz / 1/2 cup)

Method

- Heat oven to 180°C (350°F). Line the bottom of a rectangular baking dish with screwpine leaves. Top with bread slices.
- Sprinkle chopped palm sugar over and between bread slices.
- Using an electric whisk, whisk eggs with castor sugar until thick and creamy. Stir in coconut milk mixture.
- Pour mixture into prepared baking dish. Leave for 15 minutes for the bread to soak up the custard.
- Cover baking dish with aluminium foil and place in a large roasting pan. Fill pan with hot water to reach about 5 cm (2 in) up the sides of baking dish to obtain gentle heating.
- Bake for about 30 minutes or until custard sets. Remove foil and continue to bake for another 15 minutes or so to brown crust.
- In the meantime, prepare syrup. Dissolve palm sugar in water until a thick pouring consistency is reached. Stir in coconut milk, then drizzle all over warm pudding and serve.

Note

You can make a bread pudding with any sort of leftover bread. If using dense, rustic bread however, do increase the amount of custard used. I like to cut down the amount of coconut milk used, by mixing it with soy milk, but you could also use low-fat milk.

Baked Pumpkin and
Coconut Pudding

(For 10)

A no-flour dessert that takes its inspiration from an old-fashioned baked dessert *kuih bengka*, made from tapioca (cassava). Here, I use pumpkin which is lighter and more easily obtainable.

Ingredients

Pumpkin	1, about 1 kg (2 lb 3 oz)
Brown sugar	1 cup
Eggs	2
Grated coconut	1 cup
Coconut milk	1 litre (32 fl oz / 4 cups)
Salt	a pinch
Screwpine (*pandan*) leaves	2, cut into pieces
Butter	2 Tbsp, softened

Method

* Preheat oven to 180°C (350°F).
* Peel pumpkin and shred using a grater. Mix shredded pumpkin with brown sugar, eggs, grated coconut, coconut milk and salt.
* Grease a casserole dish using a butter spray. Place screwpine leaves at the bottom of casserole dish and spoon mixture carefully into prepared dish.
* Dot butter on top of mixture, then place into oven and bake for 50 minutes or until top is golden. If preferred, serve with crème fraîche or whipped cream.

Tip

You can reduce the saturated fat content in this recipe by substituting coconut milk with soy or low-fat milk. Instead of using 1 litre (32 fl oz / 4 cups) coconut milk, use 500 ml (16 fl oz / 2 cups) soy or low-fat milk and 500 ml (16 fl oz / 2 cups) coconut milk. Those who prefer less sweet tastes may also reduce the amount of brown sugar in the recipe to $2/3$ cup.

ONE-DISH

I love one-dish meals. They help me concentrate my mind on just that one dish, which means less confusion, fuss and bother!

No wonder families of old used to turn out pots of just curry chicken, *laksa lemak* (coconut noodles) or *mee siam* (spicy vermicelli) whenever they had big gatherings and everybody was happy to eat just that one dish.

This chapter continues that tradition but with recipes that offer a difference with a twist.

While the name says it all—you get a balanced meal of protein (meat or fish), carbohydrates (rice or noodles) and vitamins and fibre (vegetables) on a plate—it is the convenience rather than the nutritional aspects that appeals to me.

Everything is cooked in one pan, sometimes even served in that one same utensil, which means less to clean and no need to think of what other ways to cook the vegetables or the rice.

Besides, everyone loves these uncomplicated meals because they are delicious in their own right.

Unlike in the past, however, when cooks were sometimes forced to concentrate on just one dish such as *popiah* (spring rolls), because it demanded a lot of back-breaking effort, I have unashamedly incorporated modern kitchen conveniences into the preparation work, rendering such recipes a breeze to make.

In the recipe for *nasi ulam,* for example, all the age-old injunctions of finely shredding the herbs into hair-like strips by hand are firmly thrown out. No more heart-stopping slogging here or in other recipes indeed!

I have also gone a step further in that I now imitate the Western fashion of offering a roast sometimes for weekend get-togethers. They are also one-dish meals, albeit in a roasting pan. And yes, I do rely on an oven unlike many Asian cooks where the oven is still a less than popular appliance. Even today, there are families who do not own an oven and some, steeped in yin and yang principles, believe that roasting increases body 'heatiness'.

Despite the Western style presentations, these dishes—such as the roast pork and chicken and, indeed, many other roast recipes throughout the book—retain the Asian flavours, for truly we love them best!

Lethoke

(For 6–8)

A hot and sour Southeast Asian main course salad that has noodles and rice, and indeed, all the essential food groups on one plate. And to think it is actually an old Burmese recipe. If you prefer it lighter, omit the carbohydrates. I offer just rice in the recipe.

Ingredients

Round white cabbage	1/2 head
Carrots	2
Cucumbers	2
Potatoes	3–4
Fish cakes	4, large
Firm bean curd (*tau kwa*)	4 pieces
Cooked rice	5–6 cups

Garnish

Dried prawns (shrimps)	1 cup
Sliced shallots	1 cup
Chilli powder	

Dressing

Shallot oil	250 ml (8 fl oz / 1 cup), leftover from frying shallots
Fish sauce	125 ml (4 fl oz / 1/2 cup)
Tamarind juice	250 ml (8 fl oz / 1 cup), from mixing 1 Tbsp tamarind paste with 250 ml (8 fl oz / 1 cup) water, then strained
Sugar	1 tsp

Method

- Prepare garnishes a few days ahead. Wash dried prawns under a tap and drain well. Pound or process until fine. Heat 2 Tbsp oil in a pan and fry pounded dried prawns until golden brown. Drain and leave to cool before storing in a bottle until needed.

- Heat 250 ml (8 fl oz / 1 cup) oil and fry sliced shallots until crisp and brown. Drain and leave to cool before storing in a bottle until needed. Reserve shallot oil.

- On the day itself, prepare vegetables. Wash and finely shred cabbage, carrots and cucumbers (remove soft cores first). Boil potatoes, then peel and slice. Fry fish cakes and bean curd whole until lightly brown, then cut into cubes.

- Prepare dressing by mixing together shallot oil, fish sauce, strained tamarind juice and sugar. Taste to adjust seasoning. It should be rich, salty, sweet and sour all at once.

- Place shredded vegetables, fried fish cakes and bean curd, garnishes and cooked rice on separate plates. Allow guests to help themselves to the salad ingredients, drizzle some dressing over and mix well before taking a mouthful of the most beguiling salad ever.

Note

The idea is a do-it-yourself salad with diners picking as much or as little of the components as they like. Traditionally, even the dressing is served in its separate components. While I have used cabbage, carrots and cucumbers, the Burmese would instead offer green papaya, glass vermicelli and green gram powder.

Tom Yam **Bouillabaisse**
(For 8)

This broth marries hot-sour Thai flavours with a French bouillabaisse. I came up with it when I was desperate for a one-dish meal to feed friends who were coming only late at night. And what could be better than a gutsy soup with everything in it?

Ingredients

A selection of seafood (eg. prawns (shrimps), fish, mussels, clams and squids)	1–1.5 kg (2 lb 3 oz–3 lb 4$^{1}/_{2}$ oz)
Cooking oil	125 ml (4 fl oz / $^{1}/_{2}$ cup)
Onions	6, large, peeled and chopped
Bottled *tom yam* paste	4 Tbsp
Kaffir lime leaves	4
Lemon grass	3 stalks, discard tough outer layers and use only bottom white part, cut into short lengths
Tomatoes	2, chopped
White wine (optional)	
Water	
Baby corn cobs	16
Green capsicums (bell peppers)	4, cored and cut into quarters
Mushrooms (any kind)	8–10
Coconut milk	125 ml (4 fl oz / $^{1}/_{2}$ cup)

Method

❖ If using prawns, leave unshelled. Wash and drain. If using fish steaks, cut into smaller pieces. If using mussels and clams, scrub clean. If using squids, remove ink sacs, beak and quill. Clean and cut rest of squid into rings.

❖ Heat oil and sauté onions until translucent. Add *tom yam* paste and fry for a few minutes together with lime leaves and lemon grass until fragrant. Add chopped tomatoes.

❖ When oil rises to the surface of fried spices, add cleaned seafood, adding fish last. Stir gently to ensure even mix of spices.

❖ If you have some white wine on hand, add a generous lug, then top up with water to just cover seafood. Cover and cook for about 15 minutes or until shellfish turns pink.

❖ Discard any unopened clams and mussels. Add corn, capsicums, mushrooms and coconut milk. Taste to adjust seasoning. Remove from heat.

❖ Serve bouillabaisse in bowls with rice, noodles or bread.

Note

Timing is of the essence here. Make sure you do not overcook the seafood. And do not worry about fully cooking the vegetables—they will cook in the residual heat of the pot. Use the coconut milk as you would cream, stirring it in only at the end.

Roast Chicken
Marinated in Wine Lees
(For 6–8)

This is a Chinese-style roast chicken that relies on an unusual but delightful paste in its marinade. The paste is the residue from making rice wine. Bright red in colour, it is naturally wine-like in flavour, adding to its appeal. You'll find it sold in jars at certain supermarkets.

Ingredients

Chicken	1, about 1.5 kg (3 lb 4½ oz), visible fat removed
Shallots	10, peeled and left whole
Garlic	10, peeled and left whole
Taiwanese cabbage (*xiao bai cai*)	5–6 bunches, boiled

Marinade

Red wine lees paste	4 Tbsp
Light soy sauce	1 tsp
Honey	1 Tbsp
Salt	½ tsp
Vegetable oil	1 tsp

Method

* Preheat oven to 200°C (400°F) (fan-assisted).

* Combine marinade ingredients. Use a fork to stir and emulsify mixture.

* Carefully slip your fingers under skin of chicken to loosen it. Rub marinade under and over skin, and into cavity of chicken as well. Leave some marinade aside for gravy.

* Place chicken on a large roasting pan and loosely cover with foil. Roast for 30 minutes.

* Turn heat down to 150°C (300°F). Add whole shallots and garlic and roast uncovered for another 20 minutes or so. Pierce chicken with a skewer in the thickest part of the thigh. If juices run clear, chicken is ready. If not, cook for another few minutes.

* Place whole chicken on a bed of boiled cabbage, then scatter with roasted shallots and garlic.

* Prepare gravy. Skim fat from juices left in roasting pan. Add about 250 ml (8 fl oz / 1 cup) water and leftover marinade to the pan and simmer on top of the stove, using a spatula to scrape loose any leavings in roasting pan. Taste to adjust seasoning.

* Serve roast chicken with gravy on the side.

Five-spice Roast Pork

(For 6–8)

I love this Chinese roast pork, rubbed with traditional five-spice powder but presented Western style. I roast the meat on thick onion rings and throw in potatoes as well into the pan, creating a meal in a roasting pan.

Ingredients

Salt	1 Tbsp
Ground white pepper	2 tsp
Five-spice powder	1 Tbsp
Belly pork	1 kg (2 lb 3 oz), with rind, uncut
Vegetable oil	
Onions	4, large, peeled and cut into 2-cm (1-in) thick slices
Potatoes	4–5, peeled and cut into 8–10 pieces

Method

❖ Preheat oven to 200°C (400°F) (fan-assisted).

❖ Dry-fry salt, pepper and five-spice powder in a wok for a few minutes. Rub roasted seasoning all over pork. Leave uncovered in the refrigerator overnight. This effectively dries out pork skin and ensures a crisp crackling.

❖ Before roasting, score rind in several places and rub oil all over it.

❖ Place pork, skin side up, on onion slices in a roasting tray to allow the heat to circulate all around meat.

❖ Roast for 10 minutes to sear meat, then turn heat down to 160°C (325°F). Throw in potatoes, rubbed first with oil and salt, and continue to roast for 1 hour. Remove potatoes when golden.

❖ Increase heat to maximum 250°C (475°F) and roast for 15 minutes or until skin crackles.

❖ Remove pork from oven, rest for 30 minutes, then slice. Serve with roasted onions and potatoes on the side.

Note

To get that crackling finish:

• Drying, even in the refrigerator, ensures a crisp skin during roasting, because it removes all the moisture. Any moisture left on the surface of the meat will steam the meat before it has a chance to brown.

• The temperature of the oven is also important. Browning only occurs above 150°C (300°F), which is why the last blast at maximum heat of 250°C (475°F) (fan-assisted) is imperative for a spectacular crackling.

• The balance you have to strike is between a crisp finish and the meat drying out. So choose a fatty piece of meat that will self-baste in its own fat.

• Finally, you have to salt the meat liberally. Salt draws some of the meat's juices to the surface allowing the meat to caramelise and brown.

Sek Bak

(For 6–8)

A traditional braised pork dish. I serve it like a Chinese *bollito misto*, that Italian dish of boiled meats. Following the Eurasian custom of serving *sek bak* as a salad, I also make a salad from the dish but with only squid, fish cake, mint and coriander (cilantro) to cut through the richness.

Ingredients

Lean belly pork	500 g (1 lb 1¹/₂ oz)
Pork neck	500 g (1 lb 1¹/₂ oz)
Pig or veal tongue	1
Cloves	4–5
Star anise	8–10
Cooking oil	2 Tbsp
Shallots	5–6, peeled and chopped
Garlic	3–4 cloves, peeled and chopped
Salt	¹/₂ tsp
Sugar	1 Tbsp
Thick dark soy sauce	2 Tbsp
Cooked pig's tripe	200 g (7 oz), available at the supermarket
Firm bean curd (*tau kwa*)	2 pieces
Lettuce	

Marinade

Thick dark soy sauce	1 Tbsp
Light soy sauce	1 Tbsp
Honey	1 tsp
Five-spice powder	1 tsp

Salad

Five-spice meat rolls (*ngor hiang*)	2, available from the supermarket
Fried fish cakes	2
Squids	4, cleaned and boiled
Cucumbers	2
Coriander leaves (cilantro)	a bunch
Mint leaves	a bunch

Dressing

Bottled chilli-garlic sauce	1 cup
Limes	2, squeezed for juice
Stew gravy	2–3 Tbsp
Chopped onion	
Sliced red and green chillies	

Method

- Combine ingredients for marinade and place whole belly pork and pork neck in to marinate. Leave for a few hours, if not overnight, covered in the refrigerator.
- Simmer pig or veal tongue whole in water in another pot, with cloves and 4–5 star anise, for 1 hour. When it cools, peel off skin, which should come off easily.
- Heat oil in a wok and sauté chopped shallots and garlic until golden. Add remaining star anise and fry until fragrant, then brown marinated pork.
- Add remaining marinade to wok with 500 ml (16 fl oz / 2 cups) to 750 ml (24 fl oz / 3 cups) water and simmer for a few hours or until meats are tender.
- Halfway through, season with salt, sugar and dark soy sauce. Add cooked tongue, tripe and bean curd.
- Keep heat gentle throughout and keep turning meats around in sauce. If sauce gets too thick, add some water. You want a rich and dark gravy with a hint of sweetness.
- Prepare salad. Lightly fry five-spice meat rolls and fish cakes, then drain. Cut meat rolls, fish cakes, squids and cucumbers (cores removed) into cubes. Add a handful of chopped coriander and mint leaves.
- Prepare dressing. Mix bottled chilli-garlic sauce with lime juice, then thin down with stew gravy. Top with chopped onion and sliced red and green chillies.
- To serve, slice belly pork, pork neck, bean curd, tripe and tongue and place on a plate. Pour gravy over. Serve with salad, sprinkled with dressing. If preferred, offer white rice or Chinese steamed buns on the side.

Note

From this spiced stew, you can also obtain various well-loved dishes. Use only belly pork and stuff into Chinese steamed buns to get *kong bak pau;* chop up bits of everything in the pot to fill fried firm bean curd squares for *hor pau* or add pig's offal to the pot and serve the meats, sliced, with a bowl of soft watery *kway teow* (flat rice noodles) for *kway chap*.

Easy Nasi Ulam

(For 8)

This is actually a Malay herb rice recipe which the Nyonyas adapted and called their own. I used to hanker for its clean green taste, imbued with the fragrance of fresh herbs. Now I can turn it out in a jiffy as I realised that the shredded herbs are like an Asian pesto that can be easily processed in a food chopper.

Ingredients

Toppings

Pounded dried prawns (shrimps)	4 Tbsp, or bottled chilli prawn (shrimp) floss
Skinned grated coconut	1 cup
Salt	
Kaffir lime leaves	3, finely shredded
Spanish mackerel (*tenggiri batang*)	2–3 steaks, each about 200 g (7 oz)
Fried shallots	
Prawns (shrimps)	300 g (10^1/$_2$ oz), small
Cucumber	1, peeled
Long beans	100 g
Cooked rice	8 cups
Red chillies	2, sliced

Herb paste

Young kaffir lime leaves	20
Young turmeric leaves (*daun kunyit*)	2
Lesser galangal leaves (*daun cekur*)	4
Thai sweet basil leaves (*daun selasih*)	10
Laksa leaves (*daun kesum*)	10
Belacan (dried prawn (shrimp) paste)	1 Tbsp, toasted
Vegetable oil	4 Tbsp
Salt	a pinch

Method

- Separately roast pounded dried prawns and grated coconut, mixed with a pinch of salt and 1 shredded lime leaf, in a slow 100°C (200°F) oven until browned.

- Steam fish slices, seasoned with ^{1}/$_2$ tsp salt, until cooked. This will take about 15 minutes. Cool, then flake fish, removing skin and bones. Steam prawns in the same way, then peel.

- In the meantime, prepare herbs for chopping. Wash, dry and use only leaves. Place herbs in a food processor together with toasted *belacan* and oil. Add salt and chop until fine. Set aside.

- Core cucumber and dice. Cut long beans into fine dice and scald. (You can also cook it for 2 minutes on High in the microwave oven.)

- Place cooked rice in a large bowl or tray. Add flaked fish and diced vegetables. Mix in herb paste. Toss well to ensure that it is well mixed.

- Top with cooked prawns, browned coconut, fried shallots and browned dried prawns. Garnish with sliced red chillies and remaining shredded kaffir lime leaves to serve.

Note

These fresh herbs can be bought from Asian markets. In Singapore, purchase them from the Geylang Serai or Tekka markets. The most characteristic scent of this herb rice comes from the kaffir lime leaves, so you can omit the other leaves if you cannot find them. Choose younger leaves for a smoother paste although the flavour will not be affected if older leaves are used. And, if you have *sambal belacan*, toasted prawn (shrimp) paste and chilli, do offer it as well.

Healthy Laksa

(For 6–8)

Another favourite made healthy by replacing coconut milk with soy milk. You can hardly tell the difference from the taste, as it is the spices and herbs, rather than the milk that give the noodles its well-loved flavour.

Ingredients

Prawns (shrimps)	100 g (3¹/₂ oz), leave shells on
Vegetable oil	1 Tbsp
Lemon grass	1 stalk, discard tough outer layers and use only bottom white portion, bruised with the back of a knife
Dried prawns (shrimps)	1 Tbsp, rinsed
Unsweetened soy or coconut milk	1 litre (32 fl oz / 4 cups), or use a mixture of both
Salt	1 Tbsp
Sugar	1 tsp
Fresh thick rice vermicelli (*bee hoon*)	400 g (14 oz)
Fish cakes	4, sliced
Bean sprouts	100 g (3¹/₂ oz), tailed and lightly boiled
Laksa leaves (*daun kesum*)	1 bunch, stems discarded and finely shredded

Spice mixture

Dried red chillies	5, softened first in water
Belacan (dried prawn (shrimp) paste)	1 tsp
Peeled shallots	¹/₂ cup
Galangal (*lengkuas*)	5 slices, peeled
Ground turmeric	¹/₂ tsp, or 1 thumb-sized knob fresh turmeric
Ground coriander	1 Tbsp

Method

- Place ingredients for spice mixture into a food processor and chop until fine.

- Bring 250 ml (8 fl oz / 1 cup) water to the boil and cook prawns until just pink. When cool, peel prawns and leave aside, together with prawn stock.

- Heat oil in a pot large enough for the gravy. When hot, brown spice mixture, together with lemon grass, until fragrant. Add a little prawn stock from time to time to prevent burning.

- Add dried prawns and sauté for a few minutes. Add 750 ml (24 fl oz / 3 cups) to 1 litre (32 fl oz / 4 cups) water and bring gravy to the boil, then add soy or coconut milk. Reduce heat to prevent curdling. Season with salt and sugar, or to taste.

- In the meantime, scald rice vermicelli with hot water and divide equally among 6 bowls. Top with prawns, fish cake, bean sprouts and *laksa* leaves. Pour hot gravy over and serve immediately.

Tip

Instead of making the spice mixture from scratch, you might be able to find bottled *laska* paste in the supermarkets. Simply refresh with fresh *laska* leaves and lemon grass. Soy milk is very rich in flavour. If preferred, you can thin it down with water. If it curdles, use a wire whisk to break up the lumps.

Pumpkin Coconut Rice

(For 6–8)

This is my take on *nasi lemak* or coconut-flavoured rice. I add *sambal* and pumpkin to the rice and offer a grilled tamarind fish to cut through the sweetness. Add some cucumber, if you like, for some fresh crunch.

Ingredients

Butternut pumpkin	1, about 1 kg (2 lb 3 oz)
Long-grain rice	3 cups
Cooking oil	1 Tbsp
Onion	1, peeled and chopped
Bottled Nyonya *sambal* chilli paste	2 Tbsp (*see* Note)
Screwpine (*pandan*) leaf	1
Coconut milk	250 ml (8 fl oz / 1 cup)
Kaffir lime leaves (optional)	
Cucumber slices (optional)	

Fish

Tamarind pulp	2 Tbsp
Spanish mackerel (*tenggiri batang*)	6 steaks
Salt	1 Tbsp
Sugar	1 tsp

Method

- Rub tamarind paste into fish steaks. Add salt and sugar, then leave to marinate, covered, for at least 1 hour or overnight in the refrigerator.
- Peel and cut pumpkin into large cubes. To make this easier, cook whole pumpkin in the microwave oven on High for 5 minutes to soften it before cutting.
- Wash, then drain rice grains.
- Heat oil in a wok and fry onion. Add Nyonya chilli paste, then rice and stir until grains are well-coated with chilli.
- Add pumpkin pieces and continue to cook for a couple of minutes, stirring all the time.
- Transfer rice mixture to a rice cooker. Add 500 ml (16 fl oz / 2 cups) water, screwpine leaf and cook until rice is tender. At the end of cooking, add coconut milk and stir thoroughly. Switch rice cooker off and leave covered for a while to allow rice grains to absorb flavours.
- When rice is ready, heat grill. Coat marinated fish steaks with a little vegetable oil. Place fish on the topmost level to cook until browned in parts. It should take just 3–5 minutes on either side.
- To serve, spoon rice onto a large platter and top with grilled fish. Garnish with kaffir lime leaves and serve with cucumber slices as desired.

Note

Bottled Nyonya *sambal* chilli paste is available from the supermarkets. In Singapore, Glory and Sinalong are reliable brands. If you are uncertain, check the ingredients label. They should include chilli, prawns, onions, sugar, salt and sometimes lemon grass. If not, make up your own: Place 1 cup shallots, 4 dried chillies, 2 fresh red chillies, 1 Tbsp *belacan* (dried prawn (shrimp) paste), 1 Tbsp sugar and 1/2 tsp salt in a food processor and chop until fine.

Roti John with
Chicken, Corn Kernels and Green Chillies

(For 6–8)

An old favourite takes on Mexican flavours. Instead of just egg and onion, I have added chicken, corn kernels and green chilli to the mixture. Lovely for brunch or lunch or, indeed, anytime you want a light meal!

Ingredients

Cooking oil	
Onion	1, large, peeled and chopped
Minced chicken	100 g (3^1/$_2$ oz)
Corn kernels	^{1}/$_2$ cup
Salt	^{1}/$_2$ tsp
Eggs	4, beaten
Green chillies	4, sliced
Ground white pepper	to taste
Baguette or French loaf	1, large

59
MAD
ABOUT
FOOD
THE COOKBOOK

Method

❖ Heat 1 Tbsp oil in a pan and sauté onions until translucent. Add minced chicken, then corn kernels. Season with a pinch of salt. Mix thoroughly, then remove from pan and cool.

❖ Combine eggs and cooled chicken mixture, then add green chillies. Season with remaining salt and pepper to taste.

❖ Slice bread lengthwise into halves. Cut each half crosswise into 4 or 5 equal sections.

❖ Heat a frying pan (skillet), then add 4–5 Tbsp oil to prevent sticking. Dip bread, cut side down, into egg mixture. Spoon some meat onto bread and quickly place it, meat side down, into hot pan.

❖ Press down hard on bread for egg mixture to stick. Leave for a couple of minutes, then, using tongs, turn bread over to brown other side for another 2 minutes or so.

❖ Remove from pan and place on kitchen paper to drain. Serve immediately with a green salad on the side and a plate of sweet chilli sauce as a dip as desired.

❖ You can also leave bread slices covered with foil in the refrigerator until needed and refresh in a slow 150°C (300°F) oven for 10 minutes or so just before serving.

Note

Instead of fresh chicken mince, you can also use cooked leftovers—roast chicken, beef or lamb—or even canned tuna in the egg mixture. For a vegetarian version, omit the meat and substitute with diced capsicums (bell peppers) and black olives.

QUICK

I know the days when you do not feel like cooking and yet cannot bear the thought of going out to buy food. Or perhaps you want to entertain but do not have the energy to pull out the stops.

I have such days. And sadly, they may be every day! That is when I resort to my repertoire of quick dishes, all achievable within 15 minutes and many requiring only store cupboard ingredients. They are dishes that require little thinking, minimal effort and yet result in lots of flavour.

Some of these recipes do not call for any sort of cooking whatsoever, merely assembly, as in the marinated salmon and tomato salad that unusually marries both Italian and Japanese flavours.

Others require at best a toss in a heated pan. The two pasta dishes fall within this category and yet these are hardly unsophisticated food—they derive their notes from the fragrance of the torch ginger bud in one and exploit the Asian addiction to salted fish, fried crisp and dry, in another.

Quick they may be, but these are no ho-hum dishes. They could easily be trotted out for family and guests alike, as they all have a twist that refreshes.

I love my tofu dressed cold, for example, with fresh coriander crisp-fried to make a fragrant oil dressing, while that old favourite *chye tow kway* may assume a rather sophisticated guise to surprise the most jaded palate.

Even ice cream, that perennial fall back for dessert, can be made surprising as you can see in my suggestion for ice cream with *chendol* or *bubor cha cha* flavours.

Do you have 15 minutes? That is all it takes, I promise, for a dish that is simple and yet leaves you craving for more.

Updated Chye Tow Kway

(For 6–8)

Traditional radish cakes are chopped up first, then fried in lots of oil with preserved radish (*chye poh*) and garlic. Here, I sear large slices of radish cakes and finish the dish off with a lavish garlic and radish topping. This way, the dish uses less fat, is stylish in its presentation and is still yummy!

Ingredients

Cooking oil	2 Tbsp
Chopped garlic	2 Tbsp
Chopped preserved radish (*chye poh*)	½ cup
Steamed radish cake	500 g (1 lb 1½ oz), cut into slices

Garnish

Chopped spring onion (scallion)

Dried chilli flakes

Method

❖ Heat oil in a frying pan (skillet), then sauté garlic until fragrant. Add preserved radish and fry until golden. This can be done ahead of time and kept covered in the refrigerator until needed.

❖ Using an oil spray, lightly coat another frying pan or a ridged grill pan with oil. Heat until smoking, then brown radish cakes until nicely seared.

❖ Lay browned cakes on a plate and scatter warmed garlic and preserved radish topping over.

❖ Garnish with chopped spring onions and chilli flakes.

Note

You can find steamed radish cakes in the refrigerator section of Asian food shops or supermarkets. For a change, use yam cakes, but top with fried small dried prawns (shrimps) and shallots instead.

Deep-fried Shishito Peppers with Seaweed and Dried Bonito Flakes

(For 6–8)

These large Japanese chillies are not spicy. Instead, they are crunchy and turn sweet after deep-frying. This is an appetiser that takes just minutes to prepare.

Ingredients

Vegetable oil	250 ml (8 fl oz / 1 cup)
Shishito peppers (Japanese green chillies)	20–25
Light soy sauce	2 tsp
Dried bonito flakes	1/2 cup
Japanese seaweed (*nori*)	1–2 sheets, cut into strips
Lemon	1, cut into quarters

Method

* Heat oil in a frying pan (skillet) until smoking hot. Fry whole chillies in batches (this ensures that they fry rather than steam) until they are well seared. Remove and drain chillies on absorbent paper.

* Place seared chillies on a plate, drizzle with light soy sauce and scatter bonito flakes and seaweed strips over. Serve immediately with a squeeze of lemon.

Note

Shishito peppers are available from Japanese supermarkets. If unavailable, substitute with pale green Thai banana chillies or green capsicums (bell peppers).

Bean Curd with
Fresh Coriander Sauce

(For 8 as part of a meal)

Again, a quick dish, stunning in its simplicity. Here, cold bean curd is dressed with a beguiling green oil made from crisp-fried coriander leaves.

Ingredients

Silken bean curd (tofu)	3 cakes
Coriander leaves (cilantro)	2 large bunches
Vegetable oil	125 ml (4 fl oz / ½ cup)
Salt	1½ tsp

Method

- Remove bean curd from packaging and leave for a few hours on a strainer in the refrigerator to drain.
- In the meantime, make coriander sauce. Wash and dry coriander leaves, then chop.
- Heat oil in a wok. When smoking hot, fry chopped coriander leaves until they begin to turn crisp. It should not take more than a few minutes, if the oil has been heated well. Add salt to season.
- Remove crisp leaves and oil, which is now full of flavour, from hot wok and cool. When ready to serve, place cold bean curd on a plate and top with green coriander oil and leaves.

Note

- It is important to heat the oil before frying the herb to ensure a crisp finish.
- The sauce can be made in advance and stored in the refrigerator until needed. In fact, I do this as a matter of course for leftover coriander leaves. It can also be used to flavour fish or pork.

Marinated Scallops, Salmon and Tomato

(For 8)

This marinated fish unusually combines Japanese and Italian flavours. While scallop is included in this recipe, you can keep costs down by just using salmon.

Ingredients

Sashimi-quality salmon	300 g (10$\frac{1}{2}$ oz)
Sashimi-quality raw scallops	4–5
Ripe tomatoes	5

Dressing

Rice vinegar	1 tsp
Olive oil	4 Tbsp
Light soy sauce	2 Tbsp
Salt	a pinch
Sugar	a pinch
Onion	1, peeled and chopped

Garnish

Chopped parsley (optional)

Method

- Slice salmon, scallop and tomatoes. Leave covered in the refrigerator until needed.
- Combine dressing ingredients and set aside for about 1 hour for flavours to develop. Taste and adjust seasoning accordingly.
- Divide chilled seafood and tomato into 8 portions, arranging salmon then scallops on top of tomato slices. Drizzle with dressing.
- Garnish, if desired, with chopped parsley. Serve immediately.

Note

When eating seafood raw, always buy sashimi-quality seafood. To save time, you can even buy sliced sashimi, then store it in the refrigerator and use on the day itself.

Turmeric **Prawns**

(For 10 as part of a meal)

This is an extremely easy recipe, for it takes just minutes to prepare and uses only three main ingredients—turmeric, salt and prawns (shrimps). And yet, it is a lavish dish, thanks to the large prawns used.

Ingredients

Large prawns (shrimps)	500–600 g (1 lb 1$\frac{1}{2}$ oz–1 lb 5 oz)
Ground turmeric	1 tsp
Salt	1 Tbsp
Vegetable oil	1 Tbsp + 125 ml (4 fl oz / $\frac{1}{2}$ cup) for frying
Lime (optional)	1, cut into wedges

Method

- Buy the freshest prawns you can find. I like them on the large side as there is more bite in them.

- Leave shells on to keep in the juices but slit shells at the top so that you can devein prawns, if necessary, and also to allow the spices to penetrate. Leave whiskers flowing for they add to the final presentation.

- Rub ground turmeric, salt and 1 Tbsp oil into prawns. Allow them to sit in the marinade for 30 minutes, covered, in the refrigerator.

- Heat oil for frying in a wok. When smoking, add prawns, a few at a time, to allow them to sear and brown properly. (This step is important, as a wok that is not hot enough will cause the prawns to steam rather than fry.)

- When golden, remove from wok. Serve immediately with wedges of lime on the side, if desired.

Note

A member of the ginger family, the turmeric root is knobbly like ordinary ginger and it has an almost pungent, acrid taste that softens after cooking.

Mrs Verma's Egg Pasta
with Torch Ginger Bud
(For 6–8)

If you like the idea of soft, yielding noodles permeated with the scent of torch ginger bud and enriched gently with Parmesan cheese, this is the dish for you.

Ingredients

Torch ginger buds (*bunga kantan*)	2–3
Olive oil	4 Tbsp
Chopped garlic	1 Tbsp
Chilli powder	1 tsp
Salt	1 tsp
Dried egg tagliatelle	500 g (1 lb 1¹/₂ oz)
Parmesan cheese	

Method

❖ Pull off the tough outer petals of ginger buds and discard. Slice finely from the tip down. The slivers will break up easily.

❖ Heat olive oil in a pan. Lightly brown chopped garlic over a slow fire, stirring occasionally until fragrant. Add chilli powder, salt and half the chopped ginger buds. Stir for 1 minute, then remove from heat.

❖ Boil tagliatelle in plenty of salted water. It should take just 5 minutes, as egg pasta does not take long to cook. Drain, reserving 250 ml (8 fl oz / 1 cup) pasta water for use later.

❖ Add pasta to stir-fried ingredients and toss gently until thoroughly mixed. Top with shavings of Parmesan cheese and toss to allow cheese to melt in the residual heat. If pasta seems too dry, stir in some of the reserved pasta water.

❖ Garnish with remaining chopped ginger buds.

Tip

Forget about those packets of ready shredded Parmesan cheese and buy a wedge instead. Shave off curls of cheese with a potato peeler or grater just before serving to obtain maximum flavour.

Spaghetti with Lemon Grass, Chilli and Salted Fish

(For 6–8)

Asian salted fish is found in this pasta sauce. The idea is not so startling when one remembers that salted anchovies are used in Italian recipes. This is a combination that truly appeals to Asian taste buds.

Ingredients

Dried spaghetti	500 g (1 lb 1½ oz)
Salted threadfin (*ikan kurau*)	150 g (5½ oz)
Olive oil	4 Tbsp
Onion	1, peeled and roughly chopped
Ripe red tomatoes	4, roughly chopped
Lemon grass	1 stalk, discard tough outer layers and use only white bottom portion, cut into rounds
Salt	a pinch
Red chillies	2–4, sliced
Thai sweet basil leaves (*daun selasih*)	

Method

- Boil pasta in a large pot of salted water.
- Wash salted fish quickly under a running tap and slice it as thinly as you can.
- Heat 2 Tbsp olive oil in a pan and brown salted fish over low heat. When crisp, remove from oil and set aside.
- Add more oil if needed and reheat pan. Sauté onion, tomatoes and lemon grass until fragrant. Season with a pinch of salt.
- The pasta should be ready by now. Drain and place in a large bowl.
- Cover pasta with sautéed onions, tomatoes and lemon grass and garnish with browned salted fish, red chillies and basil leaves. Toss and serve immediately.

Salted Egg Cucumber Salad

(For 10)

This is a simple cucumber salad that has been teamed with salted duck's egg to make it a real hit! Great when eaten with curries.

Ingredients

Salted duck's eggs	4
Cucumbers	4
Onion	1, peeled and thinly sliced
Red chillies	2, sliced
Limes	4, squeezed for juice
Salt	a pinch or to taste
Sugar	1 Tbsp

Method

- Scrape black earth coating from eggs with a knife. Wash eggs clean, then hard-boil, covered, in a small pot of water.
- Remove core of cucumbers and slice thickly on the diagonal. Place in a salad bowl and top with sliced onion and chillies.
- Drain eggs and shell under a running tap if they are still hot. Cut into wedges and add to bowl.
- Dress with lime juice, salt and sugar. If you like, add shredded lime zest for a fresh lime flavour. Toss before serving.

Roasted **Spicy Cauliflower**
(For 8)

Even those who don't like vegetables will be tempted by this spiced cauliflower dish.

Ingredients

Cauliflower	1–2 heads, about 500 g (1 lb 1$\frac{1}{2}$ oz)
Olive oil	2 Tbsp
Salt	1 tsp
Chilli powder	2 tsp or more
Chopped coriander leaves (cilantro)	

Method

- Preheat oven to 200°C (400°F) (fan-assisted).
- Break cauliflower up into fairly large florets. Place florets on a baking tray and drizzle oil over.
- Sprinkle salt and chilli powder (more if you like it spicy) over florets and rub in evenly.
- Roast for about 20 minutes or until vegetable looks charred in parts. Serve hot or at room temperature. Garnish as desired with chopped coriander.

Tip

A bold addition of oil and salt ensures a full-bodied taste, while a sprinkling of spices or fresh herbs adds flavour. Most of us are too timid with spicing and salting of vegetables and so our vegetables end up with a pallid result, which is probably why cooked vegetables have a bad name.

Chendol **Ice Cream**
(For 8)

This is a frozen version of the Asian dessert where all the flavours of *chendol*—green flour strips, red beans and palm sugar—are spooned over coconut ice cream. But don't bother making coconut ice cream from scratch, I offer a quicker way!

Ingredients

Vanilla ice cream	250 g (9 oz)
Coconut milk	250 ml (8 fl oz / 1 cup)
Chopped palm sugar (*gula* Melaka)	1 cup
Water	250 ml (8 fl oz / 1 cup)
Rum	1 Tbsp
Green *chendol* strips	1 packet, 300 g (10¹/₂ oz), available from the refrigerator section of supermarkets
Sweetened red beans	1 small tin, 430 g (11¹/₂ oz), available from Japanese sections of supermarkets or boil 1 cup red beans until soft and add sugar to sweeten

Method

- Allow ice cream to melt slightly and stir coconut milk into it. Cover and re-freeze until solid.
- Prepare palm sugar syrup. Place chopped palm sugar into a small pot. Add water and rum and heat gently until sugar melts into a brown syrup. Strain into a cup and leave aside.
- To assemble, scoop out 1–2 scoops coconut ice cream and place in a glass. Top with 2 tsp green *chendol* strips. (If necessary, break a green *chendol* strip to test and see if it has hardened. If it has, place *chendol* strips in a microwave-safe container, cover with water and heat for about 1 minute on High in the microwave oven. Leave to cool, then drain before use.)
- Add 1 Tbsp sweetened red beans. Finally, drizzle some rum-flavoured palm sugar syrup over and serve immediately.

Tip

You can ring in a change by offering *bubor cha cha* ice cream! Just top coconut ice cream with boiled sweet potato and yam cubes, colourful flour cubes (available from wet markets) and perhaps a crisp-dried jackfruit slice, obtainable in packets from the supermarket.

Avocado Mousse with
Palm Sugar and Young Coconut
(For 8)

This is just avocado squeezed from the skin of the fruit straight into a blender and mixed with coconut juice, coconut milk and sugar. A delicious mousse that does not have to rely on cream for richness.

Ingredients

Ripe avocados	8
Lemon	1, squeezed for juice
Young coconut	1, for juice and flesh
Coconut milk	250 ml (8 fl oz / 1 cup)
Chopped palm sugar (*gula* Melaka)	1 cup
Water	250 ml (8 fl oz / 1 cup)
Rum	1 Tbsp

Method

- Cut ends off avocados and squeeze pulp right into the blender. Add lemon juice. Pour in coconut juice and coconut milk and blend until smooth.

- Prepare palm sugar syrup. Place chopped palm sugar into a small pot. Add water and rum and heat gently until sugar melts into a brown syrup. Strain into a cup and leave aside.

- Divide mousse among 8 dessert cups. Top with coconut flesh and drizzle generously with palm sugar syrup.

Note

It is important for the avocados to be ripe and also to have lemon juice on hand as it prevents the avocado pulp from darkening due to oxidation. You can add more coconut milk if you prefer it richer. The aim is to achieve a soft, yielding mousse.

Five-minute Trifle with
Strawberries and Lemon Curd

(For 4 or more)

A dessert that takes just 5 minutes to prepare and yet, is delicious with the richness of cream and the crunch of nuts, cut through with strawberries and lemon curd.

Ingredients

Strawberries	16–20, hulled and cut into halves
Sugar	2 Tbsp
Brandy	4 Tbsp
Whipping cream	250 ml (8 fl oz / 1 cup)
Plain butter cake	4 cups, cut into cubes
Lemon curd	
Peanut brittle	1 piece, chopped

Method

❖ Sprinkle strawberries with sugar and brandy and leave to marinate in the refrigerator for a couple of hours.

❖ Using a whisk, whip cream until soft peaks form. Leave in the refrigerator until needed.

❖ To assemble trifle, place some cake at the bottom of a glass, spoon some brandy-soaked strawberries over, then add 1–2 spoonfuls of lemon curd, followed by a layer of whipped cream. Sprinkle with peanut brittle. Place in the refrigerator to chill until serving time.

Note

• You can buy lemon curd in bottles from the supermarket or gourmet shops.

• Plain butter cake is best for this recipe, but you can also use fruit cake or sugee cake as desired.

LOW FAT

Our mothers would have been surprised, but low-fat food is here to stay.

More and more people are becoming conscious of the effect of too much fat, salt and sugar on their health and are more restrained now about adding such ingredients to the pot. Unlike in the past, when cooks thought nothing of using lard and coconut milk in their food, these days, lard is definitely out and vegetable oil, and more recently olive oil, is in.

The trend is so entrenched that even market stallholders will skin and remove the fat from chickens routinely for customers and even ask if they would prefer leaner cuts of streaky pork or mince!

Such concerns even dictate the choice of cooking methods. Deep-frying, for example, is seriously getting outmoded in home kitchens, though admittedly, this may be more likely due to the inconvenience of splatter rather than health.

While I do follow the principles of healthy cooking as much as possible, I am on the whole rather relaxed about them and will include butter, cheese, lard, salt and even coconut milk in my cooking. To me, moderation is the better principle, and delicious food continues to be my aim.

But delicious eating is quite easily achievable in low-fat cooking simply because of the top-notch produce asked for in these recipes. If you want to cook foods using the barest of seasonings, you need quality fish, meat and vegetables.

And that is the secret.

Fish and meat raised in sympathetic environments, and vegetables grown organically and then harvested in their prime cannot help but taste delicious.

And so the recipes found in this chapter are included firstly because they make for good eating. It is only incidental that they also incorporate the principles of healthy cooking!

Put in another way, low-fat food need not be boring as these recipes show. Even traditional dishes such as *laksa* (pg 54) and Hokkien *mee* (pg 98) can be made healthy quite easily, and without sacrificing too much of their characteristic flavour!

Green Chilli **Seared Tuna**

(For 4–6 as a starter)

It can't get simpler than this. Just fresh tuna, seared on the outside but raw on the inside, dressed with a fresh lemon-flavoured soy sauce. It takes just minutes, yet is always welcome at the table because nothing beats the taste of truly fresh fish.

Ingredients

Sashimi-quality tuna	300 g (10$\frac{1}{2}$ oz) (choose a piece that is evenly thick from end to end to ensure even browning)
Green chillies	2
Lemon	1, squeezed for juice
Light soy sauce	4 Tbsp
Sesame oil	1 tsp

Method

- Heat a cast-iron frying pan (skillet) until hot. Lightly spray pan with oil using an oil spray. When smoking hot, place whole piece of tuna onto pan to sear. After a few minutes, turn fish over to sear the other side.

- You can determine the degree of doneness by watching the colour change at the cut ends of the fish. You want fish that is seared on the outside but raw on the inside.

- Remove from heat. When cool, slice fish into 1-cm ($\frac{1}{2}$-in) thick slices. Arrange on a serving plate.

- Slice green chillies. Place a sliced chilli on each tuna slice.

- Make up a citrus-flavoured soy sauce by adding lemon juice to light soy sauce. Add sesame oil and adjust according to taste. Just before serving, drizzle sauce over seared fish slices.

Tip

To prevent fish sticking to the pan, heat pan thoroughly before spraying with oil. Oil sprays are available from the supermarket. I used an olive oil spray.

Snow White Chawan Mushi

(For 4)

A light and savoury white custard filled with nice surprises such as seafood, chicken and vegetables. The secret lies in the stock used, for it essentially flavours the silky custard.

Ingredients

Dashi, bonito or chicken stock	750 ml (24 fl oz / 3 cups)
Egg whites	3
Mirin (sweetened rice wine)	1 Tbsp
Salt	1/2 tsp
Light soy sauce	1/2 tsp or to taste
Carrot	1/2, sliced
Fresh soy beans or *edamame*	a handful, removed from pods
Fresh shiitake mushrooms	4, quartered
Boneless chicken thigh	1, cut into cubes and marinated with sake to taste

90
MAD
ABOUT
FOOD
THE COOKBOOK

Method

- To make *dashi* or bonito stock, bring to the boil a pot of water with a 5 cm (2-in) square piece of dried seaweed (also known as *konbu* or *kombu*) and 1/2 cup dried bonito flakes. Strain and cool. *Konbu* and dried bonito flakes are available from Japanese supermarkets. Otherwise, use ready-made stock, chicken or even powdered *dashi*, also obtainable from supermarkets, in which case, adjust seasoning to taste.

- Beat egg whites just enough to break them up. Don't beat too vigorously for you might incorporate too much air into the mixture, causing little air bubbles to form in the final custard.

- Add cooled stock to beaten egg whites, beating gently all the time with a fork to prevent whites from curdling.

- Flavour egg mixture with *mirin*, salt and soy sauce.

- Divide carrot slices, soy beans or edamame, mushrooms and chicken cubes evenly among 4 heatproof (flameproof) ramekins. Pour egg mixture slowly over ingredients to ensure that they do not float to the top.

- Bring a wok half full of water to the boil. When steaming hot, place 4 ramekins, covered first with aluminium foil, on a metal rack in the wok. Steam covered over medium heat for 8–10 minutes. The soy beans or edamame and mushrooms will float to the surface during steaming.

- The custard is done if a toothpick inserted into the centre comes out clean. Serve immediately.

Tip

Some people describe *chawan mushi* as an egg soup since the moisture from the other ingredients causes the final custard to become rather moist. To prepare a smooth and silky *chawan mushi*, steam over gentle heat so that the mixture never boils and so retains its silky texture.

New-fangled
Raw Fish Salad

(For 10 as a starter)

This is my take on our famed New Year raw fish salad where I use more fish than usual and less oil and sugar. Although the dressing uses only 1 tsp oil, the salad offers an explosion of flavours, colours and textures.

Ingredients

Sashimi-quality salmon	500 g (1 lb 1¹/₂ oz)
Baby red radishes	2, sliced into rounds
Shallots	4–5, peeled and sliced
Japanese cucumber	1, sliced into rounds
Coriander leaves (cilantro)	a few
Red chillies	2–3, sliced
Young ginger	1 thumb-sized knob, peeled and cut into thin strips
Kaffir lime	1, grated for zest
Red salmon roe (optional)	3 Tbsp

Dressing

Lime juice	3 Tbsp
Light soy sauce	1 Tbsp
Sugar	1 tsp
Sesame oil	1 tsp
Salt	a pinch
Ground white pepper	to taste

Method

- Place salmon in the freezer for 10–15 minutes to firm up the flesh, then slice as thinly as you can and store in the refrigerator until needed. Otherwise, buy ready-sliced sashimi fish from the sashimi counter at Japanese supermarkets.

- Combine dressing ingredients and stir well. Taste to adjust seasoning.

- Assemble salad by placing fish slices on a plate. Top with slices of radish, shallot and cucumber and garnish with coriander leaves, chilli slices, ginger strips and kaffir lime zest. Scatter salmon roe, if using, on top.

- Just before serving, pour dressing over and toss (*lo hei*)!

Tea-smoked **Red Snapper**
(For 8 as part of a meal)

This smoked fish is soft and silky and yet impregnated with the fragrant smoke of tea. It would do as well as a cold starter for a Western meal, served then with sweet vinegared mustard.

Ingredients

Whole red snapper	4, each about 20-cm (8-in) long, cleaned
Black Chinese tea leaves	2 cups
Sugar	2 Tbsp

Marinade

Dark soy sauce	2 Tbsp
Rice wine	2 Tbsp
Sugar	1 Tbsp
Salt	1 tsp or to taste

Method

❖ Mix together dark soy sauce, rice wine, sugar and salt to make up marinade. Rub it all over snapper and refrigerate for 30 minutes to marinate.

❖ Line the bottom of a cast-iron wok, large enough to hold a fish or 2 on a steaming tray, with aluminium foil. Scatter tea leaves mixed with sugar on the foil. Position steamer stand in wok and heat wok, covered, over a hot fire until tea leaves begin smoking.

❖ Place 1–2 fish on a steaming tray and place on stand. Cover wok and reduce heat to medium. Leave fish to smoke for about 15 minutes or until cooked. The fish is cooked if the eyes have turned opaque and the flesh flakes easily with a fork. Remove from heat. Repeat this process for remaining fish.

❖ Fillet fish and serve either hot or cold, with freshly squeezed lemon juice, plain mayonnaise or sweet vinegared mustard.

Note

You could prepare this dish using an oven, but smoking in a wok is more efficient because of the confined space. When using a wok to smoke the fish, choose a heavy cast-iron wok (with a well-fitted cover), otherwise you will blacken the bottom of a less hardy pan.

Fish **Satay**

(For 8)

Again, full of flavour, but with little fat. Here, fish is rubbed with the spices associated with Malay satay, then grilled. A little coconut milk is sprinkled on top to moisten the fish while cooking.

Ingredients

Bamboo skewers	8–10
Fish steaks (Spanish mackerel (*tenggiri batang*) or snapper)	5, large
Ground turmeric	1 tsp
Ground coriander	1 tsp
Ground cumin	1 tsp
Salt	1 tsp or to taste
Coconut milk	2 Tbsp
Bottled satay peanut sauce	
Kaffir lime leaves	2–3, shredded

Method

- Soak bamboo skewers in water for at least 15 minutes to prevent them burning when under the grill.
- Cut fish into even-sized cubes to get about 24–30 pieces.
- Toss fish cubes with ground turmeric, coriander, cumin and salt. Drizzle with coconut milk.
- Thread fish, about 3–4 cubes to a skewer. Cover and refrigerate for 10 minutes before grilling.
- Heat grill. Place skewers on the topmost level and cook first on one side, then the other, until fish is barely browned. It should take about 3 minutes on each side.
- Serve immediately with bottled satay peanut sauce warmed through with shredded kaffir lime leaves, or plain with just a squeeze of lime juice.

Hokkien **Mee**

(For 6–8)

Believe it or not, this is a low-fat version of fried Hokkien *mee*, otherwise known as Rochore *mee*. Instead of being fried, the noodles are bathed in a flavourful pork and seafood stock. My family loves it especially when it is served with copious amounts of sliced red chilli.

Ingredients

Lean pork	150 g (5^1/$_2$ oz)
Small prawns	150 g (5^1/$_2$ oz)
Squids	3–4, medium-sized
Cooking oil	1 tsp
Chopped garlic	1 Tbsp
Shallots	3–4, peeled and sliced
Fish sauce	1–2 Tbsp
Sugar	1 tsp
Salt	^{1}/$_2$ tsp
Ground white pepper	to taste
Bean sprouts	300 g (10^1/$_2$ oz)
Fresh thick yellow noodles (Hokkien noodles)	500 g (1 lb 1^1/$_2$ oz)
Chinese chives (*ku cai*)	100 g (3^1/$_2$ oz), cut into short lengths

Garnish

Sliced red chillies
Crisp-fried shallots

Method

- Trim all visible fat from pork. Parboil pork in a pot filled with 1.2–1.5 litres (40–48 fl oz / 5–6 cups) water. Remove pork, cool and cut into strips. Set pork strips aside for use later. Skim fat from stock and reserve it.

- Peel prawns, reserving shells. Boil prawn shells in pork stock for about 20 minutes. Strain stock.

- Remove ink sacs, beaks and quills from squids and boil whole. Cut squid tubes into rings and set aside.

- Heat oil in a large wok. Sauté garlic and shallots until fragrant and softened but not browned.

- Add pork strips and peeled prawns and fry until prawns turn pink. Add squid and pour in stock. Season with fish sauce, sugar, salt and pepper to taste.

- Bring to the boil, move ingredients to one side of wok and add bean sprouts. Return to the boil, then add noodles and chives. Cover noodles with cooked ingredients and toss to mix well. Serve immediately with generous amounts of sliced red chillies and crisp-fried shallots.

Note

Don't worry about what seems like copious amounts of gravy. The noodles will absorb the gravy quickly.

Pumpkin and Cashew Nut Curry

(For 10 as part of a meal)

There is a plethora of boiled curries and far from being bland and boring, they are delicious and silky like this one, where I add pumpkin to the pot to sweeten it.

Ingredients

Raw whole cashew nuts	2 cups
Butternut pumpkin	1, medium-sized
Ground turmeric	1 tsp
Chilli powder	1 tsp
Ground coriander	1 Tbsp
Garam masala	1 tsp
Coconut milk (optional)	125 ml (4 fl oz / 1/2 cup)
Salt	1 Tbsp
Green chillies	2
Cooking oil	2 Tbsp
Shallots	4–5, peeled and sliced
Bombay duck (Indian dried fish) or any dried flat fish	2–3 pieces
Lemon	1/2

100
MAD
ABOUT
FOOD
THE COOKBOOK

Method

❖ Soak raw cashew nuts for a couple of hours to soften. Soften pumpkin in the microwave oven for a few minutes on High to make it easier to handle. Peel and cut pumpkin into large cubes.

❖ Place ground turmeric, chilli powder and ground coriander in a pot. Add drained cashew nuts and pumpkin cubes. Add water until it covers half the pumpkin cubes and bring to the boil. Simmer for about 15 minutes or until pumpkin is tender.

❖ Add garam masala and coconut milk, if using. Season with salt and pop in green chillies, snapped into pieces.

❖ As a final dressing, heat oil and fry sliced shallots until brown. Remove and drain. Fry Bombay duck or dried fish until crisp, then drain and chop. Top curry with fried fish and fried shallots. Squeeze some lemon juice over before serving. Garnish as desired.

Note

This dish can be easily made vegetarian by omitting the dried fish topping.

Grilled Aubergines with
Green Chilli Herb Dressing
(For 8–10)

This dressed roasted aubergine (eggplant/brinjal) dish has an Indo-Chinese flavour, due to the fish sauce used. Flavoured oil adds richness, chilli livens up the palate, while fresh coriander and spring onions (scallions) titillate the senses.

Ingredients

Aubergines (eggplants/brinjals)	5–6
Coriander leaves (cilantro)	1 small sprig
Green chillies	2–3
Spring onions (scallions)	2
Vegetable oil	2 Tbsp
Fish sauce	1 Tbsp
Lemon	1/2

Method

- Check if there are worms in aubergines by splitting aubergines in half lengthwise. Cut off any worm-eaten bits, a common problem with this vegetable.

- Heat grill until hot. Use an oil spray to lightly oil aubergines and place on a pan on the uppermost rung under the grill. Cook until skin is burnt in parts.

- In the meantime, chop coriander leaves, green chillies and spring onions. Place in a bowl, add vegetable oil and fish sauce (or light soy sauce, if you want it vegetarian).

- Place grilled aubergine halves on a plate, pour green chilli herb dressing over, then squeeze lemon juice over to serve. You can also chill this dish in the refrigerator if you prefer to eat it cold.

Burmese Pennywort and Tomato Salad

(For 6)

Indian pennywort, a wild herb eaten in countries such as Myanmar and Sri Lanka, has a unique and unforgettable flavour. The faintly bitter coin-shaped leaves are delicious in a salad with aromatics such as crisp-fried shallots and garlic, dried prawns (shrimp) and toasted nuts.

Ingredients

Tomatoes	4–5, thickly sliced
Onion	1, large, peeled and finely sliced
Indian pennywort leaves (*gotu kola*)	1 bunch, shredded to fill 2 cups
Mint leaves	a few sprigs
Coriander leaves (cilantro)	a few sprigs

Garnish

Chopped roasted peanuts	2 Tbsp
Crisp-fried shallots	
Crisp-fried garlic	
Pounded dried prawns (shrimps)	2 Tbsp
Shallot or garlic oil (from frying shallots or garlic)	1 tsp
Limes	2–3, squeezed for juice
Sugar	1/2 tsp
Salt	1 tsp

Method

- Arrange tomatoes on a plate and top with finely sliced onion.
- Shred pennywort leaves by rolling them up tightly and using a knife to cut through the roll finely.
- Scatter shredded pennywort leaves over tomatoes and onion. Scatter mint and coriander leaves over.
- Garnish generously with roasted peanuts, fried shallots, fried garlic and pounded dried prawns.
- Add shallot or garlic oil, lime juice, sugar and salt over the lot. Toss well and serve immediately.

Note

Pennywort grows wild in Sri Lanka and Myanmar. In Singapore, you can purchase the herb from Tekka market at Serangoon Road. Look for the stalls which sell all kinds of hard-to-find vegetables, located at the far end of the market. Omit the use of dried prawn (shrimp), if you want a vegetarian dish.

Mixed Fruit Salad with Thai Flavours

(For 4–6)

I discovered this sweet, sour and welcomingly, juicy salad in Chiang Mai, Thailand. Eaten at the end of a hot and dusty day, it really hits the spot.

Ingredients

Guava (seedless, if possible)	1/2
Starfruit	1/2
Thai rose apples (*jambu*)	2
Pineapple	1 slice
Red grapes	a handful, halved and seeded
Cherry tomatoes	a handful, halved
Coriander leaves (cilantro) and root	1 small sprig
Small dried prawns (shrimps)	1 Tbsp, rinsed
Shallots	4–5, peeled and thinly sliced
Red bird's eye chillies	2–3, sliced
Chopped peanut/sesame brittle	2 Tbsp, roughly chopped

Dressing

Lemon	1, squeezed for juice
Orange	1/2, squeezed for juice
Fish sauce	1 Tbsp or to taste
Sugar	1 Tbsp or to taste
Ground white pepper	to taste
Salt	to taste

Method

- Prepare a basin of salted water (using 1 tsp salt). Peel guava and trim tough rinds from starfruit. Cut fruit, except for grapes and cherry tomatoes, into large cubes and soak in salted water to prevent fruit from turning brown.
- Pluck leaves from coriander and set aside. Chop coriander stems and root and reserve for use in dressing.
- Prepare dressing. Place chopped coriander root and stems in a bowl. Add lemon juice, orange juice, fish sauce, sugar, pepper and salt. Stir well to mix. Taste and adjust seasoning, if needed, but do remember that extra sweetness will come from the nut brittle. You want a balance of sour, sweet and salty flavours.
- Place mixed fruit into a glass bowl. Top with dried prawns, shallots, chillies, brittle and coriander leaves.
- Pour dressing over and toss at the table.

Note

I have chosen to use mostly Asian fruits in this recipe, but you can substitute with fruit such as green apple, honeydew melon and strawberries. Just remember, you want a bit of tartness and crunch to give some liveliness to the salad. Omit dried prawns (shrimp) and substitute salt for fish sauce to make this dish vegetarian.

Mango Soup with Pomelo Sacs

(For 4)

This is truly a low-fat dessert and is so refreshing, especially after a heavy meal. And it can be easily whipped up in a blender!

Ingredients

Ripe mangoes	4, large
Vodka	125 ml (4 fl oz / ½ cup) or to taste
Sugar syrup	2 Tbsp
Cold water	125 ml (4 fl oz / ½ cup)
Pomelo or grapefruit segments	4

Garnish

Mint leaves

Method

- Peel mangoes and cut flesh into pieces. Blend (process) mango together with vodka, syrup and cold water into a purée.
- Peel pomelo or grapefruit segments and separate sacs within.
- Serve blended mango in bowls, topped with pomelo or grapefruit sacs. Garnish with mint leaves.

Tip

This makes a thick 'soup'. If you want a lighter dessert, just add water to it. But do remember to add more syrup to sweeten it and yes, more vodka too!

Wine Jelly **with Two Berries**
(For 10)

It is hard to describe this fat-free dessert as guiltless, as it has at least half a bottle of wine in it! It is, however, especially beautiful when made in a clear glass bowl for it allows the colour of the berries to shine through.

Ingredients

Water	500 ml (16 fl oz / 2 cups)
White wine	500 ml (16 fl oz / 2 cups)
Gelatine powder	1^1/$_3$ Tbsp
Castor (superfine) sugar	220 g (7^3/$_4$ oz / 1 cup)
Lemon	^{1}/$_2$, squeezed for juice
Strawberries	1 cup, hulled
Blueberries	1 cup

111
MAD
ABOUT
FOOD
THE COOKBOOK

Method

- Combine water and wine. Place half of this mixture into a saucepan, then stir in gelatine powder, sugar and lemon juice. Heat gently until sugar is melted. (There is no need to bring the mixture to the boil unless you want to boil off the alcohol. In this case, do not halve the liquid and skip the next step.)

- Add remaining wine-water mixture. Added later, it ensures more of a kick!

- Wash berries quickly under a tap so as not to wash away the flavour. Place berries into a clear, large glass bowl or several smaller glasses. Pour in gelatine mixture. The berries will float.

- Chill, covered, in the refrigerator until set. The gelatine will set to a soft quivering jelly. If you like a firmer set, add an additional 1 tsp gelatine powder to the mix.

OCCASION

When I am entertaining at home, I like to pick dishes that create a buzz around the table.

And so, it could be pasta with an unusual Asian ingredient such as *laksa* pesto or a roast with Asian flavours as seared beef dressed with flavoured oil. Even if something traditional like Teochew oyster omelette (*or luak*) is on the menu, I like to deconstruct it to make the presentation more surprising.

But whatever the menu, I like to serve the food Western style, simply because it is so much easier. Just three or four courses and you are done! Of course, for larger groups of people, buffets still make the best sense and such ideas can be found in the chapter, Family.

Despite the special touches, most of these recipes are uncomplicated, or at least demand only limited attention, and several can be done ahead of time. After all, feeding your friends is supposed to be fun and who wants the role of a hassled host/hostess?

But even if I am serving the simplest of food, a little attention goes a long way. I will take the trouble to present it on a pretty plate, for example, or think of unexpected ways of serving it.

Why not, then, hand out individual Chinese spoons when offering Burmese tea leaf salad, or merely dish out the food on an oversized platter? Such touches bring a sense of celebration to the table!

Spicy Tuna Dip
with Rice Crackers
(For 10)

This spicy tuna dip and the following *cencaluk* dip, done ahead of time, will create a sensation at parties, for they have unusual Asian flavours. Great while waiting for the perennial late-comers to arrive!

Ingredients

Vegetable oil	1 Tbsp
Onion	1, peeled and chopped
Thai red curry paste	2 tsp
Coconut milk	100 ml (3 fl oz / ³/₈ cup)
Tuna in oil	1 can, 180 g (6¹/₂ oz)
Sugar	1 tsp
Unsalted mini rice cakes	1–2 packets (Get these from the health food sections of supermarkets. You need at least 20 pieces.)
Kaffir lime leaves	1–2 finely shredded

Method

❖ Heat oil in a pan and sauté onion gently until soft but not browned. Add red curry paste and stir until everything is fragrant.

❖ Keeping heat low, add coconut milk, entire contents of canned tuna and sugar. Allow to warm through.

❖ Serve in a large bowl, topped with some shredded kaffir lime leaves and rice cakes on the side.

Tip

If you prefer, substitute the rice crackers with unsalted wheat crackers. Thai red curry paste is available in bottles from the supermarket. You can also use bottled *sambal belacan* instead of Thai red curry paste, if desired.

Cencaluk Dip
with Young Lady's Fingers
(For 10)

Here, the classic combination of *cencaluk* (salted prawn sauce) with onions and chilli is married with the creaminess of yoghurt to obtain a rich, yet robust Asian flavoured dip.

Ingredients

Lady's fingers (okra)	20, choose young ones
Shredded kaffir lime leaves (optional)	
Shallot (optional)	1, peeled and sliced

Dip

Cencaluk (salted prawns (shrimp) sauce)	2 Tbsp
Shallots	2–3, peeled and thinly sliced
Red chillies	1–2, sliced
Yoghurt	200 g (7 oz)
Sugar	to taste

Method

- Mix together dip ingredients, leaving aside some sliced chilli for garnish. Adjust seasoning according to taste. It should be salty, sweet and a tad tart.

- If lady's fingers are small, leave them whole, otherwise cut into 2 or 3. Bring a pot of water to the boil and scald vegetable until tender (test by poking with a fork). Dunk in cold water to stop the cooking process and to retain the bright green colour. You can do this beforehand. Store in the refrigerator until needed.

- Serve boiled lady's fingers with dip on the side. Garnish as desired with shredded kaffir lime leaves and sliced shallot.

Tip

You can also serve this dip with vegetable sticks such as carrots, cucumber or boiled green beans.

Fried Black Moss Rolls
on Salad
(For 8)

Black moss or hair seaweed forms the filling for this seaweed roll. I like to serve this during Chinese New Year for the Chinese name of the seaweed—*fa cai*—sounds like the word for "good luck" in Chinese!

Ingredients

Dried black moss (*fa cai*)	40 g (1¹/₂ oz)
Store-bought scraped fish meat	2 cups
Fresh water chestnuts	10, peeled and chopped
Dried bean curd sheets	4
Vegetable oil	250 ml (8 fl oz / 1 cup)
Sweet black sauce or sweet flour sauce (*tee cheo*)	1–2 Tbsp

Salad

Mixed salad greens	
Black Chinese vinegar or balsamic vinegar	1 Tbsp
Vegetable oil	2 Tbsp
Cherry tomatoes	16, each cut into half

Method

* Soften black moss by soaking in warm water. When softened, squeeze out excess moisture, then place in a bowl. Mix with fish meat, which will already be salted, and water chestnuts.

* Wipe down bean curd sheets, which are also salted, with a damp towel to remove as much of the salt as possible. Cut sheets to get 8–10 pieces, each 20 x 10 cm (8 x 4 in).

* Spoon a portion of fish-moss mixture along the centre of each sheet. Roll up, tucking the ends under.

* Heat oil in a wok until smoking hot, then turn heat down to medium. Gently lower rolls in, and fry, 2 at a time, turning often to ensure even browning.

* Remove, drain on paper towels and when cool, cut into evenly sized pieces. Set aside.

* Toss salad leaves with vinegar and vegetable oil. Place dressed leaves on a plate. Top with black moss rolls and tomatoes, and drizzle with sweet black sauce.

Tip

You can get fish meat from the fresh fishball seller in the wet market. If unavailable, substitute with cuttlefish paste available frozen in Asian supermarkets.

Or Luak **Deconstructed**
(For 4)

In this deconstructed *or luak* or oyster omelette, the beaten eggs are cooked soft and creamy while the flour batter is fried to a crisp. The oysters are then placed raw on top, giving cold, hot and crunchy all in one mouthful.

Ingredients

Eggs	4
Fish sauce	1 tsp
Olive oil	3 Tbsp
Chopped garlic	1 tsp
Tapioca (cassava) flour	1 Tbsp
Rice flour	1 Tbsp
Water	125 ml (4 fl oz / 1/2 cup)
Salt	a pinch
Fresh raw oysters	4–8

Garnish

Dried chilli flakes
Chopped coriander leaves (cilantro)
Bottled chilli-garlic sauce
Vinegar

Method

- Beat eggs in a bowl until fluffy. Add fish sauce to season.
- Heat 1 Tbsp olive oil in a flat frying pan (skillet) until hot. Sauté garlic until fragrant, but not browned.
- Pour egg mixture into heated pan. Leave for about 10 seconds, then using a spatula, draw the liquid egg from the centre of pan to the sides. Do this 2–3 times.
- Leave omelette to cook a further 4–5 seconds until it is golden underneath. Turn over to cook the other side for another 4–5 seconds. Remove from pan and divide into 4 portions. Place on serving plates.
- Add remaining oil to pan. While it heats up, mix tapioca and rice flours with water. Add salt.
- When pan is hot, pour in flour mixture and fry over medium heat until it browns to a crisp. It should take about 5 minutes. Don't worry if it seems to be sticking. It should come away as a flat biscuit upon crisping.
- Remove, drain on paper towles and using scissors, snip into 4 portions.
- Dress each serving of omelette with 1–2 raw oysters and a toss of chilli flakes, topped with a flour crisp. Scatter chopped coriander over and serve immediately with a dressing of bottled chilli-garlic sauce thinned down with vinegar.

Stuffed Fish Maws and
Shark's Fin Soup

(For 8)

Dried fish maw tubes are stuffed with meat and garnished with red caviar to create visual interest in a classic Chinese soup.

123 MAD ABOUT FOOD THE COOKBOOK

Ingredients

Minced chicken	150 g (5^1/$_2$ oz)
Prawns (shrimps)	150 g (5^1/$_2$ oz), peeled and chopped
Fresh water chestnuts	10, peeled and chopped
Light soy sauce	1 tsp
Ground white pepper	to taste
Dried fish maws	40 g (1^1/$_2$ oz), choose the tubes, rather than the pieces
Chicken stock	2 litres (64 fl oz / 8 cups)
Cleaned and softened shredded shark's fin	1 cup, available from the refrigerator section of some supermarkets

Garnish

Red caviar

Method

- Mix together chicken, prawns and water chestnuts in a bowl. Season with soy sauce and pepper.

- Pour boiling water over dried fish maws to rid them of excess oil. When they soften, cut them into even lengths using a pair of scissors. You should obtain at least 16 pieces.

- Stuff each piece with minced chicken mixture, using a chopstick. Slick the tops of the filling with a bit of water to smoothen.

- Bring stock to the boil, lower heat and carefully place stuffed maws into stock. Cook at a bare simmer for about 15 minutes.

- Remove stuffed maws, set aside and add half the softened shark's fin to heat through. Reserve other half of shark's fin for use as garnish.

- To serve, place heated shark's fin and 2 pieces of stuffed maws in a bowl and ladle hot soup over. Garnish with reserved shark's fin and a dollop of red caviar.

Tip

Instead of fresh water chestnuts, use the canned variety to save on peeling. Chicken makes for a clean white stuffing, but you could follow tradition and use pork instead.

Babi **Guling**

(For 10)

This is Balinese roast pork, for which people would fly over to Bali to get their fix! Here, I make it with a pork shoulder rather than a whole pig, but you still get that crisp crackling finish.

Ingredients

Pork shoulder	3 kg (6 lb 9 oz)
Ground turmeric	1 tsp
Salt	1 tsp
Vegetable oil	4 Tbsp

Stuffing

Lemon grass	4 stalks, discard tough outer layers and use only bottom white portion, cut into short lengths
Shallots	1 cup, peeled
Garlic	4–5 cloves, peeled
Green chillies	4–5
Candlenuts	4–5
Kaffir lime leaves	4–5
Ginger	1 thumb-sized knob, peeled
Belacan (dried prawn (shrimp) paste)	1 Tbsp
Ground white pepper	1 tsp
Salt	1 Tbsp
Vegetable oil	250 ml (8 fl oz / 1 cup)

Spices

Ground turmeric	1/2 tsp
Ground galangal	1 tsp
Ground coriander	1 tsp

Method

- Prepare stuffing by processing all stuffing ingredients, except pepper, salt and oil, until fine. Add spices, then season with pepper and salt. Add oil to bind stuffing.

- Dry surface of pork and score skin with a knife. Rub ground turmeric and salt into skin.

- Turn pork over and coat just the meat with some stuffing mixture. If you like, roll meat up and secure with string. Leave uncovered in the refrigerator for a few hours before cooking.

- Preheat oven to 200°C (400°F) (fan-assisted).

- Remove pork from refrigerator and brush skin with oil. Roast, skin side up on a rack set on a baking tray for about 1 hour 30 minutes, or until skin is golden and meat is cooked.

- To test for doneness, insert a fork into the thickest part of the meat. The juices should run clear. If not, turn heat down to 180°C (350°F) and cook for a further 15 minutes until meat is well done. If meat looks like it is burning, protect affected areas with foil.

- To serve, remove crackling and cut into small pieces. Cut meat into desired serving-size pieces and top with spices scraped clean from tray. Serve separately.

Tip

For an extra treat, serve a Balinese *sambal* with this pork. Mix together sliced shallots, garlic and red chilli, all fried to a crisp, and serve, fragrant oil and all, with a generous dollop of salt.

Rendang **Roast**

(For 10)

I like rare roasted meat and I also like spice. This dish marries the best of two worlds, where rare meat is served with a *rendang* sauce redolent of coconut milk, tamarind and herbs.

Ingredients

Leg of lamb	1.8–2 kg (4 lb–4 lb 6 oz)
Rendang mix (Brahims brand is good)	2 small packets, each 180 g (6 oz)
Coconut milk	200 ml (6^2/$_3$ fl oz / ^{4}/$_5$ cup)
Lemon grass	4 stalks, discard tough outer layers and use only bottom white portion, finely shredded
Kaffir lime leaves	5–6, finely shredded

Sauce

Tamarind juice	125 ml (4 fl oz / ^{1}/$_2$ cup), made with 125 ml (4 fl oz / ^{1}/$_2$ cup) water and 1 tsp tamarind paste, strained
Sugar	1 Tbsp
Grated or dessicated coconut	1 cup
Kaffir lime leaves	2–3, whole
Lemon grass	1–2 stalks, discard tough outer layers and use only bottom white portion, cut into short lengths and bruised

Method

- Trim lamb of obvious fat and rub *rendang* mix into meat. Pour coconut milk over and add a scattering of lemon grass and kaffir lime leaves. Cover and leave for a couple of hours in the refrigerator.

- Preheat oven to 200°C (400°F) (fan-assisted). Place lamb, with spices scraped off, on an oiled rack in a baking pan and roast for 15 minutes. Turn down heat to 180°C (350°F) and continue cooking for 40 minutes for rare meat, 50 minutes for medium and 1 hour 30 minutes for well done.

- To make up sauce, place tamarind water into a small pot together with sugar, grated or dessicated coconut, kaffir lime leaves and lemon grass. Add leftover marinade and skimmed drippings from pan. Cook over low heat until sauce thickens into a thick marmalade.

- Remove lamb from oven and leave to rest for 20 minutes, covered with a sheet of aluminium foil.

- Serve roast sliced and drizzled with sauce or with sauce on the side. This roast goes well with white rice or Malay rice cakes (*ketupat*), available from markets and supermarkets.

Spicy Seared Beef on Asian Greens

(For 8–10)

Inspired by a Hunan meal I had in Shanghai, I made this seared beef, but dressed it with fragrant oil, spiced with lots of chillies, peppercorns and garlic, Hunan style.

Ingredients

Vegetable oil	125 ml (4 fl oz / ½ cup)
Garlic	2–3 cloves, peeled and sliced
Dried red chillies	8–10, rinsed and dried
A mix of white, black and red peppercorns	1 rounded (heaped) Tbsp
Coriander seeds	1 tsp
Beef fillet	1.5 kg (3 lb 4½ oz)
Flowering cabbage (*chye sim*) leaves	500 g (1 lb 1½ oz) or garland chrysanthemum leaves (*tang orr*), spinach (*puay leng*) or a mix of all 3 leaves
Sea salt	1 tsp
Chinese black vinegar	

Method

- Heat oil, then quickly fry garlic, dried red chillies and finally, mixed peppercorns and coriander seeds. Do this over medium heat and remove solids from hot oil after a couple of minutes to prevent them from burning. They, and the fragrant oil, become your dressing.

- Heat an oiled cast-iron frying pan (skillet). When smoking hot, sear whole piece of beef, pressing down until it is brown on each side. It should take about 5 minutes or so for each side.

- Leave beef to rest for 5 minutes, then slice thinly. This gives you very rare beef with a seared outside. Alternatively, roast in a 200°C (400°F) oven (fan-assisted) for about 30 minutes for rare, 40 minutes for medium rare and 50 minutes for well done.

- Place sliced beef on bed of washed and dried Chinese leaves, torn first into bite-sized pieces.

- Dress the lot with fragrant oil, together with whole peppercorns, coriander seeds, garlic slices and dried chillies. Sprinkle sea salt over and drizzle with Chinese black vinegar.

- If you like, toss everything together before serving to ensure the flavours are mixed through.

Tip

To complete the meal, serve this Chinese beef dish with deep-fried noodles, dusted with salt, sugar and vinegar, in good old-fashioned Teochew tradition.

Turmeric Sea Bass
in Banana Leaf
(For 8–10 as part of a meal)

You could call this a Vietnamese version of *otak otak* (spicy fish custard) but their version of turmeric-rubbed fish wrapped in banana leaves is healthier and lighter. The use of banana leaves add a touch of celebration.

Ingredients

Sea bass	1, about 600 g (1 lb 5 oz)
Ground turmeric	2 tsp
Chopped garlic	2 tsp
Salt	1 tsp
Ground black pepper	1 tsp
Fish sauce	1 Tbsp
Dried Chinese mushrooms	1/2 cup, soaked in hot water to soften, then cut into small pieces, soaking liquid reserved
Dried glass vermicelli (*tang hoon*)	1/2 cup, soaked in hot water to soften, then cut into short lengths
Banana leaves for wrapping	
Lemon wedges	

Garnish

Chopped coriander leaves (cilantro)
Sliced red chillies

131
MAD
ABOUT
FOOD
THE COOKBOOK

Method

- Make deep gashes in fish, then rub ground turmeric, chopped garlic, salt, black pepper and fish sauce into fish.

- Top fish with mushrooms and vermicelli, mixing them well into the marinade. Leave, covered, in the refrigerator for at least 30 minutes.

- When ready to cook, preheat grill. In the meantime, wash banana leaves and cut into a size convenient for wrapping. Pass leaves over an open gas flame to soften.

- Wrap fish in 2–3 layers of banana leaves, fixing them in place with either bamboo toothpicks or staples.

- Place wrapped fish under hot grill, on the topmost shelf and cook for 10 minutes on each side. Don't worry if the topmost layer of the leaf is getting burnt. This adds to the smoky flavour of the fish; just peel away the burnt leaves before serving.

- Garnish with coriander and chillies and add a squeeze of lemon before serving with plain rice and either a simple sautéed green vegetable or a salad.

Tip

Aside from banana leaves, other leaf wraps are the *rojak* leaf or *simpoh air* used for wrapping *tempe* (fermented soy bean cake), dried bamboo leaves used for wrapping glutinous rice dumplings and screwpine (*pandan*) leaves used for wrapping fried chicken. Each of these leaves imparts its own fragrance to the food, whether grilled, boiled or steamed, so take your pick!

Spaghetti **with Laksa Pesto**
(For 8–10)

Pesto is an Italian herb paste, made by using fresh basil leaves, pine nuts and garlic. Here, I use fresh *laksa* leaves (also known as Vietnamese mint, polygonum leaves or *daun kesum*) and candlenut instead for an Asian variation and it is always a hit!

Ingredients

Laksa leaves (*daun kesum*)	2 cups
Garlic	2–3 cloves, peeled
Candlenuts	8
Salt	1 tsp or to taste
Ground white pepper	to taste
Spaghetti	500 g (1 lb 1¹/₂ oz)
Olive oil	1 Tbsp
Prawns (shrimps)	6–8 large, peeled
Fish cakes	4–6, thickly sliced
Snow peas	100 g (3¹/₂ oz), strings removed

Garnish

Laksa leaves (*daun kesum*)
Coconut milk

Method

- Blend (process) *laksa* leaves, garlic and candlenuts until fine. Season with salt and pepper. Set aside.
- Cook pasta in generously salted water (using about 1 Tbsp salt) until al dente. Add some oil as well to the water to prevent pasta from sticking. Drain, reserving about 250 ml (8 fl oz / 1 cup) pasta water for use later.
- Heat olive oil in a pan and fry prawns and sliced fish cake to brown them a little. Remove from pan and reserve.
- In the same pan, stir-fry snow peas to add colour and crunch to the dish. Add prepared *laksa* paste to warm through. Toss drained pasta in sauce, adding a little of the reserved pasta water to loosen up pasta further.
- Serve immediately with seared prawns and fish cake slices on top and lots of fresh whole *laksa* leaves to garnish. Drizzle dish with coconut milk.

Note

Make extra *laksa* pesto together with some oil, and fill bottles to freeze. It makes for a convenient pasta sauce at any time.

Parpadelle **with Radicchio**
(For 8–10)

If you like bitter flavours, you will like this recipe where the bitter Italian vegetable, radicchio, is sautéed with pancetta or Italian bacon. It creates an unusual and appealing pasta sauce for it tastes surprisingly like or Chinese salted mustard greens (*kiam chye*)!

Ingredients

Olive oil	2 Tbsp
Chopped pancetta	1 cup
Chopped garlic	1 Tbsp
Onion	1, peeled and chopped
Radicchio (red chicory)	1 large head, hard core removed and shredded
Sugar	1 tsp
White wine	125 ml (4 fl oz / 1/2 cup)
Salt	1 tsp
Dried parpadelle	500 g (1 lb 1 1/2 oz)
Parmesan cheese	1/2 cup
Freshly-ground black pepper	

Garnish
Chopped parsley

Method

- Heat olive oil in a pan and sauté pancetta until lightly browned. Add garlic and onion and fry until fragrant and golden.
- Add shredded radicchio and sugar. Over high heat, toss and allow vegetable to caramelise. Add white wine and allow vegetable to wilt. Add salt and stir well. Remove from heat.
- Cook pasta in generously salted water (using about 1 Tbsp salt) until al dente. Add some oil as well to the water to prevent pasta from sticking. Drain, reserving about 250 ml (8 fl oz / 1 cup) pasta water for use later.
- Pour radicchio over drained parpadelle and sprinkle lots of parmesan cheese and black pepper on top. Toss with reserved pasta water to loosen up pasta, if necessary. Garnish with chopped parsley.

Note
Don't let the Italian terms in this recipe faze you. Pancetta is unsmoked Italian bacon, which you can substitute with bacon, and papardelle refers to wide pasta strips.

Tagliatelle with Roasted Parsnips, Tomato and Balsamic Vinegar

(For 8–10)

This is a wonderfully easy pasta sauce where all the ingredients are roasted in a pan with lots of olive oil, then used to dress the pasta. I would serve it as a first course, the way the Italians do, and follow it up with a roasted fish or meat.

Ingredients

Parsnips	6–8, medium-sized
Extra virgin olive oil	5 Tbsp
Salt	1 Tbsp
Ground black pepper	to taste
Dried tagliatelle	500 g (1 lb 1$\frac{1}{2}$ oz)
Cherry tomatoes	20, each cut in half
Balsamic vinegar	
Parmesan cheese	

Garnish
Chopped parsley

Method

- Peel parsnips and cut into cubes. Coat generously with 1 Tbsp olive oil, salt and pepper.

- Place parsnips in a roasting pan and roast in a preheated oven (fan-assisted) at 200°C (400°F) until golden on the outside but creamy on the inside. This will take about 30 minutes. Parsnips should be soft when prodded with a fork.

- While vegetables are roasting, bring a pot of salted water to the boil and cook tagliatelle (flat pasta that looks like *mee pok*) in it.

- Add tomatoes to the parsnips in the pan at the end of roasting. Drizzle with remaining olive oil.

- The tagliatelle should be nicely al dente by now, but break off a strand to test. It should still have bite. Drain.

- Add drained pasta to roasting pan and toss. Taste and adjust seasoning. Serve immediately with a drizzle of the best balsamic vinegar you can afford, generous shavings of Parmesan cheese and chopped parsley as garnish.

Burmese Tea Leaf Salad

(For 10)

Known as *lepet*, this is a hot and sour Burmese salad, made with young tea leaves. It has the sting of chilli and the sourness of lime. The Burmese serve it at the end of a rich meal to cleanse the palate for dessert, but I like to serve it as a starter instead.

Ingredients

Chinese or Japanese green tea leaves	1/2 cup
Salt	1/2 tsp
Vegetable oil	125 ml (4 fl oz / 1/2 cup)
Sesame oil	1 tsp
Limes	1–2 limes, to taste, squeezed for juice
Tomatoes	4–5, cut into cubes
Dried prawns (shrimps)	1/4 cup, rinsed and drained
Fresh garlic slivers	1/4 cup
Red or green chillies	6, sliced

Garnish

Roasted or fried nuts, seeds, dried beans and peas

Crisp-fried shallots

Mint leaves

Method

- Steep tea leaves in hot water for about 20 minutes. Strain and squeeze leaves dry. (You can keep the liquid tea for drinking, if you like.) Repeat this process 2–3 times, if you prefer the leaves less bitter.

- Using a mortar and pestle, pound softened leaves with salt and vegetable oil, a little at a time.

- Add sesame oil and lime juice according to taste. Adjust seasoning, if necessary.

- You can prepare the salad up until this point in advance. In fact, the tea leaves taste better if left marinated for a couple of days.

- To serve, place tomato cubes on a plate or on Chinese spoons and top with marinated leaves. Add dried prawns, garlic slivers and sliced chillies. Garnish with as many types of roasted condiments and fried shallots as you like, and mint leaves.

Tip

Use green tea and not black tea, which is too bitter and strong tasting. If serving *lepet* as an appetiser, a practical way of doing it is to hand out Chinese spoons for guests to help themselves from the plate.

Pandan **Crème Brûlee**
(For 8)

This is a lovely dessert that marries the rich flavour of a Nyonya *kaya* or coconut custard with the textural delight of a burnt sugar topping. It never fails to get cries of delight especially when I do the torching at the table!

Ingredients

Screwpine (*pandan*) leaves	15, roughly chopped
Water	125 ml (4 fl oz / $\frac{1}{2}$ cup)
Eggs	4, medium
Sugar	160 g ($5\frac{1}{2}$ oz / $\frac{2}{3}$ cup)
Coconut milk	500 ml (16 fl oz / 2 cups)
Extra sugar for caramelising	

Method

- Purée screwpine leaves in a blender (processor) with water. Pass liquid through a strainer to obtain juice. Set aside.

- Break eggs into a large mixing bowl, add sugar and stir, not beat, until sugar has melted and mixture thickens. You do not want to incorporate too much air into custard mixture for then it will not end up silky.

- Add coconut milk and pour strained screwpine leaf juice into coconut mixture. Stir again.

- Pour custard mixture into 8 ramekins and steam in a wok half filled with water over medium heat for 20 minutes or until custard is set.

- Leave to cool, then chill ramekins, covered with cling film, in the refrigerator.

- When ready to serve, spread 1 tsp sugar over top of custard and either grill or use a blow-torch to caramelise the top. When sugar has melted, swirl ramekin around to ensure an even spread. Serve when sugar hardens into a crisp layer.

Note

The fresh screwpine leaf juice plays an important role in this recipe. Freshly squeezed juice from the leaves of this plant from the *Pandanacea* family sends the dessert to fragrant paradise. If you want to use the custard as a spread for bread, up the sugar content to about 250 g (8³/₄ oz / 1 cup).

Roasted Pears with
Gorgonzola in a
Red Wine Sauce
(For 8)

This is a fancy dessert where a lot of the preparation can be done in advance! The red wine sauce can be made a day ahead. You can even pre-roast the pears and grill them with the cheese just before serving.

Ingredients

Red wine	750 ml (24 fl oz / 3 cups)
Sugar	250 g (8¾ oz / 1 cup)
Cinnamon stick	5-cm (2-in) length
Orange or lemon peel	a few curls
Cloves	5–6
Gorgonzola cheese	200–300 g (7–10½ oz), cut into cubes and left at room temperature to soften
Castor (superfine) sugar	3 Tbsp
Ground almonds	½ cup
Firm Bosc or D'Anjou pears	4
Freshly cracked black pepper	

Method

- Bring to the boil red wine in a small pot, together with sugar, cinnamon stick, orange or lemon peel and cloves. Cook until wine sauce turns syrupy. Cool, then cover and store in the refrigerator until needed. You can do this in advance.

- Using a fork, mix cheese with sugar (more if you have a sweet tooth) and ground almonds, then roll into a ball from which you pinch off 8 walnut-sized portions. Leave aside.

- Halve pears lengthwise and remove cores using a melon baller or metal ice cream scoop. Slice a bit off the bottom of each pear half to allow it to sit without toppling over.

- Butter a shallow baking dish, add a couple of tablespoons of water and place pears, cut sides up, in dish. Roast pears in a preheated oven (fan-assisted) at 200°C (400°F) for about 15 minutes.

- Remove from oven and place a dollop of cheese mixture into each pear hollow. Roast until cheese melts and turns brown. This will take about another 10 minutes. Serve hot.

- Drizzle with prepared red wine sauce, and grind some black pepper over the lot. Serve with ice cream for more decadence.

Note

For this dish, you can use any blue cheese that is not too strong in flavour, so as not to overpower the flavour of the pears. I have used both Gorgonzola and a New Zealand Gippsland Blue to good effect. The pears have to be brown Bosc or red D'Anjou pears, however. Both have a firm and dense flesh and are less likely to be overwhelmed by spices.

MENU SUGGESTIONS

Meet the In-laws
Tofu with Fresh Coriander Sauce (pg 66)
Babi Guling (pg 124)
A Green Salad
Avocado Mousse with Palm Sugar and Young Coconut (pg 82)

Midweek Dinner
Deep-fried Shishito Peppers with Seaweed and Dried Bonito Flakes (pg 64)
Spaghetti with Lemon Grass, Chilli and Salted Fish (pg 74)
Five-minute Trifle with Strawberries and Lemon Curd (pg 85)

Family Bash
Cencaluk Dip with Young Lady's Fingers (pg 116)
Tom Yam Bouillabaisse (pg 44)
Chendol Ice cream (pg 80)

Ladies Only
Burmese Tea Leaf Salad (pg 138)
Turmeric Sea Bass in Banana Leaf (pg 131)
Easy Nasi Ulam (pg 52)
Pandan Crème Brûlee (pg 140)

Guys Only
Green Chilli Seared Tuna (pg 88)
Tagliatelle with Roasted Parsnips, Tomatoes and Balsamic Vinegar (pg 137)
Spicy Seared Beef on Asian Greens (pg 128)
Wine Jelly with Two Berries (pg 111)

Teens Only
Roti Babi (pg 16)
Indonesian Barbecued Spare Ribs (pg 21)
Roasted Spicy Cauliflower (pg 79)
Five-minute Trifle with Strawberries and Lemon Curd (pg 85)

An Asian Tea
Spicy Tuna Dip with Rice Crackers (pg 114)
Roti John with Chicken, Corn Kernels and Green Chillies (pg 59)
Updated Chye Tow Kway (pg 63)
Lethoke (pg 42)
Coconut Bread Pudding (pg 36)

GLOSSARY OF INGREDIENTS

Basil leaves

What is commonly referred to as basil is usually Italian basil, which is widely used in Mediterranean countries and flavours everything from pasta sauces to pesto. It is sweeter and milder than the Asian basils and, like all herbs, best used fresh.

Belacan (dried prawn (shrimp) paste)

Made from pounded, salted and fermented tiny prawns called *gerago* in Malay, it is then dried and formed into cakes where the colour may vary from a dark mauve to dark brown, depending on the length of processing. *Belacan* can be used to flavour spice pastes.

Bombay duck

This is a popular dried fish found on the Indian sub-continent. It is made from drying a narrow, 15-cm (6-in) long fish called bummalo. Pungent in its dried state, it, however, makes for an addictive snack after frying and is great as a crisp aromatic topping for curries.

Brown soy bean paste (*tau cheo*)

Soy bean paste results when yellow soy beans are inoculated with a mould culture, and then left to mature in brine. Despite its name, it is a suspension of whole beans, rather than a paste. To make a paste, simply mash the beans. A full-bodied seasoning, it is more often cooked rather than used as a condiment at the table.

Butternut pumpkin

An elongated, bell-shaped pumpkin with smooth creamy-brown skin and orange flesh, the butternut pumpkin has a sweet, nutty aroma when cut. Select those with hard, thick skin and which feel heavy for their size.

Candlenuts

The raw candlenut is bitter and is believed to be toxic when uncooked. This is why it always found cooked up in a spice paste. Its role is to add richness and thickness to gravies, and it is also a traditional binding agent.

Chinese chives (*ku cai*)

Chinese chives, also called garlic chives, have flat, dark green leaves and a distinct garlicky flavour. Easily overcooked, Chinese chives should be added at the last minute to stir-fries or used as a garnish. They are also very perishable and should be used within two days of storage in the refrigerator.

Fermented black beans

A soy bean, the black bean is commonly found dried or fermented in salt. It adds a delicious burst of salty flavour to stir-fried or steamed dishes and is a classic match for fish, beef, chicken or vegetables such as capsicums (bell peppers), aubergines (eggplants/brinjals) and bitter gourd.

Galangal (*lengkuas*)

This is the underground stem or rhizome of the galangal, a member of the large tropical ginger family. Pungent and peppery in flavour, it is commonly teamed with turmeric in spice pastes when making *sambals* and curries.

Indian pennywort leaves (*gotu kola*)

Actually a medicinal herb, the young leaves with its slight bitter tang are great in salads, especially when combined with shallots and nuts. The herb is said to help improve memory and relieve the pain of arthritis, among other claims.

Kaffir limes and leaves

Nothing can beat the fragrance of the kaffir lime and its leaves. The fruit can be recognised by its lumpy skin and as it gives little juice, it is important for its zest and leaves, which are used whole in curries, to be shredded into salads or pounded into *sambal belacan*, a table condiment, for extra flavour.

Laksa leaves (*daun kesum*)

Also known as Vietnamese mint or polygonum leaves, *laksa* leaves have a pungent, sharp flavour, reminiscent of both coriander and lemon and are the fresh garnish that scents *laksa* or spicy coconut milk noodles. The leaves are best used fresh and added to dishes as garnish, as their flavour fades away and they turn dark upon cooking.

Lemon grass

Known as *serai* in Malay, this is a tropical grass that gives off a heavenly lemony fragrance and is grown for its bulbous stems. These stalks are bruised before being added into curries, sliced finely for salads or stir-fries, or cut into short lengths to be ground up in spice pastes.

Lesser galangal leaves (*daun cekur* or *kencur*)

Also known as ressurrection lily, the fresh rhizome, which belongs to the ginger family, may be cooked with vegetable or meat dishes but the tender dark green leaves of the plant, which grow close to the ground, are more often found in *nasi ulam*, a herb rice salad. These leaves are also a medicinal herb.

Mint leaves

The Asian mint with its rounded serrated leaves is one of many varieties of mint. Often used raw to flavour salads and cooked foods, mint leaves can also be infused in hot water and taken as tea. Easily bruised, they should only be added at the last minute to stir-fries or other cooked dishes, as they will darken upon cooking.

Parsnips

Parsnips are related to the carrot, except that they are creamy white, both inside and out. They have a rich, nutty flavour and were used instead of the potato in old recipes. Parsnips can be boiled, roasted or cooked in stews and soups.

Shishito peppers (Japanese green chillies)

These are sort of like a cross between green chillies and green capsicums (bell peppers). They are larger than a chilli but smaller than a capsicum and are less spicy than they look. They are best eaten grilled or deep-fried, when the heat has caramelised the sugars found in the chillies.

Tamarind pulp

The tamarind fruit is a bean-like pod, which is green when fresh and brown when ripe. It is sold in many forms—in its pod, as compressed pulp or paste or in a fine sauce. It adds a sour, tangy taste to dishes. The paste is the most convenient for you can then control the sourness and consistency with water.

Thai sweet basil leaves (*daun selasih*)

This is the green-stalked Asian variety where the scent is more delicate than its red-stalked cousin, the cinnamon basil. It is closest to the Italian basil in fragrance and is used in stir-fries, curries, soups and salads. Thai sweet basil leaves are best plucked just before use.

Torch ginger buds (*bunga kantan*)

This is the flower of another tropical ginger, generally used raw. The pale pink buds are shredded to scent salads such as *rojak*, a Malaysian salad dressed with black prawn (shrimp) paste (*haeko*), Penang *laksa* (tamarind fish noodles) and Penang *asam* fish (spicy tamarind fish).

Young turmeric leaves (*daun kunyit*)

Turmeric is a member of the tropical ginger family. The turmeric rhizome has a thin, tan-coloured skin that reveals yellow-orange flesh after peeling, giving curry its colour. The leaves are used as a food wrap, a garnish or are shredded finely to add to *nasi ulam*, a herb rice salad.

WEIGHTS AND MEASURES

Quantities for this book are given using the metric system. Standard measurements used are: 1 tsp = 5 ml, 1 Tbsp = 15 ml, 1 cup = 250 ml. All measures are level unless otherwise stated.

LIQUID AND VOLUME MEASURES

Metric	Imperial	American
5 ml	1/6 fl oz	1 tsp
10 ml	1/3 fl oz	1 dsp
15 ml	1/2 fl oz	1 Tbsp
60 ml	2 fl oz	1/4 cup (4 Tbsp)
85 ml	2 1/2 fl oz	1/3 cup
90 ml	3 fl oz	3/8 cup (6 Tbsp)
125 ml	4 fl oz	1/2 cup
180 ml	6 fl oz	3/4 cup
250 ml	8 fl oz	1 cup
300 ml	10 fl oz (1/2 pint)	1 1/4 cups
375 ml	12 fl oz	1 1/2 cups
435 ml	14 fl oz	1 3/4 cups
500 ml	16 fl oz	2 cups
625 ml	20 fl oz (1 pint)	2 1/2 cups
750 ml	24 fl oz (1 1/5 pints)	3 cups
1 litre	32 fl oz (1 3/5 pints)	4 cups
1.25 litres	40 fl oz (2 pints)	5 cups
1.5 litres	48 fl oz (2 2/5 pints)	6 cups
2.5 litres	80 fl oz (4 pints)	10 cups

DRY MEASURES

Metric	Imperial
30 g	1 ounce
45 g	1 1/2 ounces
55 g	2 ounces
70 g	2 1/2 ounces
85 g	3 ounces
100 g	3 1/2 ounces
110 g	4 ounces
125 g	4 1/2 ounces
140 g	5 ounces
280 g	10 ounces
450 g	16 ounces (1 pound)
500 g	1 pound, 1 1/2 ounces
700 g	1 1/2 pounds
800 g	1 3/4 pounds
1 kg	2 pounds, 3 ounces
1.5 kg	3 pounds, 4 1/2 ounces
2 kg	4 pounds, 6 ounces

OVEN TEMPERATURE

	°C	°F	Gas Regulo
Very slow	120	250	1
Slow	150	300	2
Moderately slow	160	325	3
Moderate	180	350	4
Moderately hot	190/200	370/400	5/6
Hot	210/220	410/440	6/7
Very hot	230	450	8
Super hot	250/290	475/550	9/10

LENGTH

Metric	Imperial
0.5 cm	1/4 inch
1 cm	1/2 inch
1.5 cm	3/4 inch
2.5 cm	1 inch

ABBREVIATION

tsp	teaspoon
Tbsp	tablespoon
g	gram
kg	kilogramme
ml	millilitre

INDEX OF RECIPES